Walter Raleigh Browne

The Inspiration of the New Testament

Walter Raleigh Browne

The Inspiration of the New Testament

ISBN/EAN: 9783337242732

Printed in Europe, USA, Canada, Australia, Japan

Cover: Foto ©Lupo / pixelio.de

More available books at **www.hansebooks.com**

THE INSPIRATION OF THE NEW TESTAMENT.

THE INSPIRATION

OF THE

NEW TESTAMENT.

BY

WALTER R. BROWNE, M.A.,

Late Fellow of Trinity College, Cambridge.

WITH A PREFACE BY

THE REV. J. P. NORRIS, D.D.

CANON OF BRISTOL.

LONDON:

C. KEGAN PAUL & CO., 1 PATERNOSTER SQUARE.

1880.

CONTENTS.

	PAGE
Preface by the Rev. Canon Norris on the teaching of the Church upon the question . . .	v

INTRODUCTION.

Limits and Character of the Enquiry . .	1
The two Limiting Theories of Inspiration .	4
Reasons for accepting the Bible's witness to itself	6

PART I.

FIRST LIMITING THEORY.—THE NATURAL .	10
Christ's utterances upon Inspiration . .	11
Mission of the Spirit to the Apostles . .	19
Inspiration, so given, extended to their Writings	26
Recapitulation of this general Evidence . .	40
Special Passages on Inspiration—1 Cor. ii. 12, 13	43
,, ,, 2 Tim. iii. 14–17	47
,, ,, 1 Pet. i. 10–12	59
,, ,, 2 Pet. i. 19	62
Objection from Silence of Scripture writers as to their own Inspiration	70
Examination into the extent of this Silence .	71

General answer to this objection	73
Special evidence from cases of Disavowal of Inspiration in 1 Cor. vii	81

PART II.

SECOND LIMITING THEORY.—THE LITERAL	106
Evidence in favour of the Theory	107
Evidence against the Theory:—	
Traces of Human Thought	119
Traces of Human Error	124

PART III.

ATTEMPT TO FIX THE LIMITS OF INSPIRATION	130
Principle suggested by Warington	131
Principle of Divine Economy	132
Four classes of Divine Dealings with Mankind	133
Application of the Principle to these classes	135
Confirmation from the three states of Inspiration to be found in the Bible	144
Cases of Direct Inspiration	145
,, Indirect ,,	147
,, Preventive ,,	149
Recapitulation and Conclusion	154

PREFACE.

In the following Essay my friend, Mr. Walter Browne, endeavours to obtain from the Holy Scriptures themselves, a definition, or at any rate a clear notion, of their inspiration.

The method is *inductive*. Passages bearing on the subject are collected and examined; and from these statements or indications, the author seeks to determine the nature and extent of the inspiration which the Bible claims for itself.

To churchmen, who wish dutifully to accept the Church's teaching in such matters, as "a witness and a keeper of Holy Writ," a prior question will suggest itself: Is not the doctrine of inspiration already determined for us, if not by the Canons, yet by the hermeneutic tradition of the Church? And, if so, ought the matter to be treated as an open question? What say the Creeds? What said the General Councils or Fathers of the undivided Church?

Now if we look through the three Creeds we find one clear and explicit statement in what is called the Nicene Creed, touching, though not covering, the subject of inspiration. "I believe in the Holy Ghost . . . Who spake by the Prophets," or rather, "through the Prophets," (τὸ λαλῆσαν διὰ τῶν προφητῶν). That by "the Prophets" here were meant the prophets of the *New* as well as of the *Old* Testament, may be inferred from the common use of the term by the Fathers of the first three centuries. Thus, we find CLEMENT OF ALEXANDRIA writing, "the Apostles may most properly be numbered among the Prophets, inasmuch as through them all equally worketh that one and the self-same Spirit." (Strom. v. c. 6). And so ORIGEN: "Both the Prophets of the Old, and the writers of the New Testament, spake by one and the same Spirit, the Holy Spirit by the providence of God, through the Divine Word, enlightening these ministers of truth, the Prophets and the Apostles." (Philocal. c. 1, p. 12). That St. Paul by the word "Prophets" in Eph. i. 20, and ii. 5, means the Christian prophets of his own day is clear, for he says that the mystery of the admission of Gentiles was not *in other ages* made known, but is *now* revealed unto His (Christ's) holy Apostles and Prophets by the "Spirit."

It is highly probable, therefore, that by "the Prophets" in this passage of the Creed, we are to understand the "holy men of God," under both Testaments, who "spake as they were moved by the Holy Ghost."

We may then very safely say that we are bound to believe, as a part of the Catholic faith, that under both

Covenants there were prophets so fully inspired by the Holy Ghost, that the Holy Ghost may be said to have spoken by their mouth.

Excepting this single statement in the Creed of the Second Council, the first four Councils are entirely silent on the subject of the Inspiration of the Scriptures.

We turn, therefore, to the literature of the early Church for incidental indications of the Church's belief: and these are abundant.

The Fathers of the first three centuries constantly speak of the Scriptures as "the Divine Scriptures," "the Oracles of God," "the Wisdom of God," "the Voice of God," "the Divine Oracles." That they believed the Apostles and Evangelists of Christ to be gifted with the same plenary inspiration as the prophets and writers of the Old Testament Scriptures, is plain from numberless passages of which the following may serve as samples. We shall observe how soon the word *Scripture*—always understood to mean *inspired Scripture*—came to be applied to the genuine writings of these Apostles and Evangelists.

Before the close of the first century, and therefore while one of the Apostles was still living, CLEMENT OF ROME writes:—"The Apostles were sent forth by Christ, as Christ by the Father. Having this commission, and being assured by the resurrection of our Lord, and established in the Gospel of God, they went forth in the full assurance of the Holy Ghost, preaching the Kingdom," c. 42.

And again, "Pore over the Scriptures, the true Scriptures of the Holy Ghost: ye know that nothing wrong, nothing counterfeit, is therein written," c. 45.

And again, in c. 47, he alludes to the Epistle which St. Paul, in the beginning of the Gospel, wrote by inspiration to the Corinthians.

Both POLYCARP and IGNATIUS pointedly disclaim for their own writings the kind of inspiration which St. Peter and St. Paul had.

JUSTIN MARTYR, writing in the middle of the second century, uses no less clear and decisive language about inspiration. In his first Apology (c. 36), he says, "When ye hear the language of the Prophets, consider that you are hearing not the words of the inspired men merely, but of the Divine Word Himself Who moves them."

In his Dialogue (§ 9), he claims for the Christian that his faith rests "not on vain fables or unproven assertions, but on discourses full of the Holy Ghost, abounding in power, fruitful in grace."

Both JUSTIN and his contemporary HIPPOLYTUS liken inspiration to a tune played upon a harp. "Such deep mysteries could never have been conceived or uttered by effort of human thought; it needed a gift descending from above on holy men, who had only to yield themselves to the energy of the Divine Spirit, which, acting upon them, as a plectrum acts on a lyre, reveals to us heavenly wisdom" (Just. Cohorts, § 8). "Being perfected by the Prophetic Spirit and honoured by the indwelling Word, they were attuned to the plectrum of the Word Himself, and made to declare the mind of God."

IRENAEUS, only a few years later in the second century, speaks of the Lord having "endued His Apostles with power to set forth the Gospel; and so through them we have learned the truth and doctrine of God. For unto them the Lord said *He that heareth you, heareth me;* and he that despiseth you despiseth *me and him that sent me.* For it is to them alone that we owe the New Testament of our salvation, which they first preached orally, and then by God's will delivered to us in Scriptures, to be the foundation and pillar of our faith. . . . For after the Lord's resurrection they were indued with the Holy Spirit's power from on high, and so acquired perfect knowledge of all that they were commissioned to declare" (iii. 1).

Then follows the famous passage in which Irenaeus points out the importance of the unbroken succession of Bishops, in order that the Church may fulfil her function as a witness and keeper of Holy Writ, implying that unless we can authenticate a Scripture as *Apostolic*, we can have no assurance of its inspiration.

"By means of this unbroken tradition reaching down to our own day, we may learn with certainty what the Apostles taught ... and the Apostles, being disciples of the Truth itself, are incapable of untruth" (iii. 5).

In another passage (ii. 28. § 2), Irenaeus anticipates that remark of Origen which Bishop Butler has made so famous, that the Author of Scripture and Nature being one and the same, we must not be surprised to find the same kind of difficulties in the former that we find in the latter.

"The holy Scriptures," he says, "are perfect, being the language of the Word and Spirit, though we may be incompetent to understand their mysteries. Nor is it surprising that it should be so in spiritual and heavenly revelations, seeing that in natural and earthly things there is so much that baffles our understanding;"—then he instances the rising of the Nile, the migrations of birds, the tides of the ocean, the changes of the weather—"As therefore in natural things some things are within our knowledge, and some things beyond it, even so in the Scriptures, which are wholly spiritual, some things by God's grace we can explain, some things we must fain leave to God, not only in this world, but possibly in the world to come, that God may be ever teaching us, and something ever remaining for us to learn.... If then, we are content to leave some things to God, we shall preserve our faith and find that all Scripture, *being given to us by God*, is ever adapting itself to our need."

We notice that in the time of Irenaeus the phrase "Holy Scripture" had come to be familiarly applied to the writings of the New, as well as of the Old Testament.

THEOPHILUS, Bishop of Antioch, in a most instructive passage, cited by Whitby and Professor Westcott, shows very clearly that when the early Fathers spoke of the writers being the *organs* of the Holy Spirit, they by no means meant that they mechanically wrote down what the Spirit dictated, but that they were filled and elevated morally and spiritually by His influence:—" The men of God being filled with the Holy Spirit, and gifted with prophecy, having inspiration and wisdom from God, were taught of Him, and became holy and just. Wherefore also they were deemed worthy to obtain this recompense, to be made the instruments or organs of God, and receive the wisdom which cometh from Him; by which wisdom they spake of the creation of the world and all other things which happened before their birth, and during their own time, and which are now being accomplished in our days; and so we are convinced that in things to come the event will be as they say." And he adds—making it plain that he is speaking of the writers of both Old and New Testaments—" The things contained in the Books of the

Prophets and in the Gospels are found to be consistent, because all the writers spake by inspiration of the one Spirit of God." (*Ad. Autol.* ii. 9, and iii. 12.)

The writings of ORIGEN abound in passages ascribing plenary inspiration to the books both of the Old and of the New Testament. He rests the proof of their inspiration on their power over the human heart, and on the fulfilment of their prophecies. The fulfilment of prophecy, seen in the course of Christianity, has placed the Inspiration of the Scriptures beyond a doubt, and raised the veil from the face of Moses. Such are the outward proofs for the unbeliever; the Christian, however, will rest his faith on the teaching of the Church. The Bible is the bulwark of the Church, and the Church its guardian. That alone is to be believed as truth, which accords with the Apostolic tradition handed down in the preaching of the Church, by order of succession from the Apostles, and even now abiding in the Churches. (Origen, *de Principiis*, iv, summarised by Professor Westcott.)

Perhaps these extracts may suffice to indicate the doctrine of inspiration as held, with remarkable unanimity, by the Fathers of the early Church. No one can fail to see that they drew a broad distinction between the inspiration of the Holy Scriptures, and such assistance as they themselves were conscious of deriving from the Holy Spirit. Thus the Church's doctrine forbids us to hold what in the following Essay is called "the Natural theory" of inspiration. On the other hand it is no less clear, that any *mechanical* theory of inspiration is excluded. From first to last the Fathers make it plain that the Holy Ghost elevated the whole mind and spirit of the inspired man. Our Holy Scriptures were not written by men who spake as mere unwilling organs, as Balaam or Caiaphas may have spoken.

Between these two extreme views any theory of inspiration must be sought that is to be in accord with the Church's teaching. But between these two limits the Church does not seem to have given us any precise definition. There seems, therefore, to be a legitimate place for such Essays as the following, seeking by an inductive process to ascertain still more nearly what Scripture teaches us on this deeply interesting question.

J. P. NORRIS.

INTRODUCTION.

WHEN we speak of a book as "Inspired" we mean that, in addition to its character as a product of the human mind, there has been "breathed into" it something from a higher and supernatural source, something for which God is directly responsible, and not man. In other words, there is in an inspired book a Divine as well as a human element. Of these elements the human (however wise and good its author may have been) is in its nature uncertain, fallible, erring; the Divine, on the other hand, is certain, stedfast, and true. It would seem therefore to be of the highest importance that we should disentangle the one from the other, be able to define the limits of each, and know exactly where one ends and the other begins. In this however, as in so many other cases, God has not given that which men would *à priori* feel certain that He would give. The distinction between the Divine and the human element in the Bible certainly does not lie on the surface; it must be discovered, if it is to be discovered at all, by patient and diligent enquiry. Now to some minds the very need of enquiry seems to prove that enquiry is wrong; and any question as to the inspiration of the Bible is looked upon as an irreverent prying into that which God has not chosen to reveal. But this assuredly is a wrong view. The deep things of God are hidden by Him, not because He chooses to keep them to Himself, but even with this very aim, that we should exercise our faith and judgment and humility in the searching of them out. In such a confidence this enquiry has been undertaken.

The subject of Inspiration may be approached from the side either of the believer or of the infidel. The treatment will differ accordingly. To the unbeliever the first enquiry must be, not as to the Inspiration, but as to the authenticity and veracity of the Book, viewed simply as a piece of literature. He will not admit the Bible as a witness to its own Inspiration, until he has convinced himself that it is a genuine work of truthful men. To attain this conviction he must appeal to external as well as internal evidence, to history, philosophy, and the experience of other religions. This proof is not here attempted. The book is addressed to those who already believe that the Bible is not only the genuine production of honest and trustworthy men, but also in some sense and to some extent, the Word of God; and are therefore prepared to accept the witness it gives of itself, as the most authentic they can obtain.

The problem before us is to fix the limits of Inspiration, to determine how much in the Bible must be treated as human, how much may be accepted as divine; and it is proposed to use mainly for this object the light thrown on the subject by the Bible itself; to examine in fact that witness, whose authority all Christians are disposed to accept.

The first requisite for such an examination must surely be to collect all the passages bearing on the subject: a requisite too often neglected, in works professing to be based on Scripture truth. In the present case this has been done for the New Testament, and the collection is given in the Appendix. The Old Testament has not been treated in the same systematic manner, (1) on account of the writer's ignorance of Hebrew, precluding anything like critical investigation; (2) because the passages bearing on Inspiration are of a much more scattered and fragmentary character; (3) because the New Testament is after all the part of the Bible on which modern Christianity mainly rests, and to which it chiefly appeals; and (4) because the Inspiration of the New Testament carries with it that of the Old Testament. For the Inspiration of the Old Testament is again and again affirmed in the New Testament.

The materials being thus collected, it remains to analyse them and determine their teaching. In this, as in all such investigations, the best course is to state at the outset the various theories which may be held on the question, and then employ the body of evidence before us to verify, or to confute, each of these in turn.

Now there are two extreme theories of Inspiration, which mark the limits of thought upon the subject. Let us examine these, and if neither of them is fully borne out by the evidence, let us then try to discover where the truth lies between them.

The first may be called the Literal theory. It asserts that the Bible was dictated word for word to the writers, who were thus mere amanuenses of the Spirit. In the original autographs therefore the Divine element was everything, the human nothing: there was no imperfection beyond that arising from the fact that the meaning was to be couched in human language, and comprehended by human intellects. The Bible is in fact, or was in its first autographs, a written message, coming as distinctly and directly from God as any of the spoken messages delivered by His prophets, and recorded in the pages of the Old Testament.

Opposed to this is the second, which may perhaps be termed the Natural theory. It may be stated thus. The Bible, or at least so much of it as modern criticism decides to be genuine, is a collection of works, historical, poetical, and devotional, written in good faith by intelligent and trustworthy men, and designed by God as a record of His dealings and relations with mankind. It was doubtless written under His direction, as all true and earnest works may be said to be; but in this direction there was nothing supernatural, nothing to distinguish the Bible in kind, at least, from the works of Augustine, Hooker, or any other religious writer, whom we may believe to have written not without the grace of God.

Under this theory the idea of a Divine element sinks in fact into that of God's ordinary providence, and perhaps it ought not to be considered a theory of Inspiration at all. It represents however the limit towards which the looser theories of Inspiration tend, and beyond which lie the rationalistic doctrines which treat the Bible as a purely human work, produced under the influences either of superstition or of fraud.

These last doctrines, as has already been stated, are not discussed in this work. A postulate is here assumed, which underlies both of the above theories, viz. that God has made a revelation of Himself to men in the person of Christ, and that the special channel, through which He has chosen to transmit the record of this revelation to successive ages, is the collection of writings which we call the Bible. Now the degree in which He has Himself thought fit to influence these writings may be questioned, and forms in fact the subject of this treatise; but, granting the postulate, the deduction seems clear, that we may confidently take the Bible's own witness as our guide in determining what the extent of that influence really is. For, if not, we must hold that the authors of the Bible may have asserted what was false as to their own Inspiration, either in self-delusion or in wilful fraud. Now, taking the first alternative, it is very difficult to believe that any sane, honest and sober-minded man should deceive himself on the point, whether he is or is not under the sensible and supernatural influence of God. And that the authors of the Bible were sane, honest, and sober-minded,—altogether different men from the mystics of mediaeval and modern times,—is sufficiently established by the internal evidence of their writings, and is in fact generally admitted at the present day, even by critics who reject their testimony. But granting such a delusion to be possible, it is clear that, when once detected, it would form an almost fatal bar to the acceptance of the author's testimony as to other facts, especially facts of a miraculous or supernatural character. Still more is this the case if we take the other alternative of wilful deceit. A man who could knowingly make false claims on so awful a subject as that of his own Inspiration, would surely be unworthy of credence on any point whatever. That God therefore should have left His words and works to be recorded by men who in that very record made for themselves a false claim to Inspiration, would imply that He had taken pains, as it were, to discredit His own revelation; which scarcely any amount of evidence could make us believe to be true. If therefore we believe that the Bible is in any sense the channel of revelation, we must logically be willing to accept with confidence whatever statements we find in it as to the Inspiration of its writers, and to take these as our guide in determining its nature and extent. This fact is stated to justify the course here taken of examining the question, almost if not entirely, by internal evidence, and to anticipate any objection that may be drawn from the impropriety of trusting to a witness's own account of himself.

Our first task then will be to examine by the evidence of the New Testament the two extreme theories we have specified, and to judge whether either of them is proved by that evidence to be the truth. If not, we shall then have to re-examine the question more closely, in order to fix the exact position which the true theory holds between these two outer limits.

We must begin then either with the Natural or the Literal theory; and the Natural is chosen for the following reason:—That theory denies that there is in the Bible any special Inspiration whatever, and it will be disproved by establishing that the Bible does claim for itself and for its authors an Inspiration altogether of a special and distinctive character. To establish this is the object of the first part of this book; and, in doing so, we shall have to review almost all the evidence, of whatever kind, which the Bible furnishes on the subject. By the time we have done this we shall be able to realise what the general teaching of the Bible is, on the question of Inspiration; it will then be comparatively a short and easy task to decide whether this teaching leads us to the acceptance of literal Inspiration, or of something falling short of this. Thus a wide view of the domain we are exploring will be presented to us at the outset, and all our work afterwards will consist in selection, criticism, and decision.

PART I.

FIRST LIMITING THEORY.—THE NATURAL.

THIS theory was stated in the Introduction as follows:—"The Bible is a collection of works, historical, poetical and devotional, written in good faith by intelligent and trustworthy men, and designed by God as a record of His dealings and relations with mankind. It was doubtless written under His direction, as all true and earnest works may be said to be; but in this direction there was nothing supernatural, nothing to distinguish the Bible from the works of Augustine, Hooker, or any other religious writer, whom we may believe to have written not without the grace of God."

We proceed to test this theory by examining the statements made on the subject in the New Testament.

THE NATURAL THEORY.

In judging of the order in which to take this evidence it is clear that we should begin with the teaching of Christ Himself, as recorded in the Gospels. For all men calling themselves Christians must hold that Christ was fully inspired, and that His decision on the question of Inspiration must be absolute and final. They must also hold that the Gospels, whether inspired or not, form at any rate a trustworthy record of Christ's teaching; for otherwise they are not only useless, but delusive and dangerous, and the whole of our faith would be wrapped in uncertainty. It is therefore of the first importance to enquire *what Christ says about Inspiration*.

To ascertain this, the passages bearing on the subject have been examined, and with the following results.

1. Christ repeatedly appeals to the Old Testament (which of course formed at that time the only written Scripture) as containing prophecies both concerning Himself and others, which prophecies must certainly be at some time or other fulfilled. Thus we have the general statement, Matt. v. 18, "Verily I say unto you, Till heaven and earth pass, one jot or one tittle shall not pass from the law, till all be fulfilled:" and, in par-

ticular instances, "The abomination of desolation, spoken of by Daniel the prophet," Mark xiii. 14. "This is He of whom it is written, Behold I send My messenger," &c., Matt. xi. 10, Luke vii. 27; "This that is written must yet be accomplished in Me," Luke xxii. 31; "Had ye believed Moses ye would have believed Me; for he wrote of Me," John v. 46. Other passages are Matt. xiii. 14; xiii. 35; xvii. 11; xxi. 42; Mark vii. 6; xi. 17; Luke iv. 21; vii. 27; xx. 17; xxiv. 25; John v. 39; vi. 45; vii. 38. This certainty of fulfilment is so strongly insisted on that the prophecy is sometimes spoken of as if it actually caused, or at least necessitated, the fulfilment of the event it foretold. Thus Luke xxiv. 44, "All things must be fulfilled which were written in the law of Moses and in the Prophets and in the Psalms concerning Me;" John xiii. 18, "But that the Scripture may be fulfilled, He that eateth bread with Me hath lifted up his heel against Me."

2. Christ appeals to the Old Testament as a treasury of moral and spiritual truth, from which lessons of belief and conduct might unerringly be drawn in all circumstances. Perhaps the clearest instance of this is the narrative of the Temptation (Matt. iv. 4–10), in which He thrice

foils the assault of the evil one by the authority of the written word: "It is written, Man shall not live by bread alone, but by every word that proceedeth out of the mouth of God." Again, Matt. xix. 4, He reproves the laxity of the marriage tie by a reference to the record of its institution: "Have ye not read that He which made them at the beginning made them male and female." Of a like character are three passages in S. Mark, xi. 17, xii. 10, xii. 29.

3. In the same discourse from which the last-mentioned passages are taken is a remarkable quotation (Mark xii. 26), found also in parallel passages of Matthew (xxii. 31) and Luke (xx. 37), "Have ye not read in the book of Moses, how in the bush God spake unto him, saying, I am the God of Abraham, and the God of Isaac, and the God of Jacob;" whence the argument is drawn that as God would not speak of Himself as having any relation to non-existent personages, therefore to those patriarchs death could not have meant annihilation; there must be a life beyond the grave. This must imply the general fact that there are depths of meaning and hidden inferences to be drawn from the Bible, such as we should not dream of looking for in any other

book; and goes far to justify many of the recondite interpretations which in the early ages of the Church were so much in vogue. A somewhat similar lesson may be drawn from another passage (Matt. ix. 13), "Go ye and learn what that meaneth, I will have mercy and not sacrifice: for I am not come to call the righteous, but sinners to repentance."

4. In another memorable passage, the narrative of Dives and Lazarus, Christ apparently refers to the Old Testament as the great persuasive to repentance and holiness, sufficient in all cases except that of wilful deafness (Luke xvi. 31): "If they hear not Moses and the prophets, neither will they be persuaded though one rose from the dead."

5. There are three parallel passages (Matt. xxii. 43, Mark xii. 35, Luke xx. 42,) in which Christ uses of David, as one of the writers of Scripture, language which certainly implies distinct Inspiration, such as we have defined it. It is true the phrase is in each case different (a circumstance we are not yet in a position to discuss). In S. Luke it is simply, "And David himself saith in the Book of Psalms, The Lord said unto my Lord," &c. Here, with no *direct* assertion of David's Inspiration, it is clear that his words

are regarded as having in them something prophetic and superhuman, rendering it necessary to find some solution for the apparent paradox which is pointed out. In the other two cases the language is more explicit. In S. Matthew it is, "How then doth David *in spirit* (ἐν Πνεύματι) call him Lord?" and in S. Mark, "For David himself said by the Holy Ghost," or rather "in the Holy Ghost"—ἐν τῷ Πνεύματι τῷ Ἁγίῳ—the preposition ἐν being the same in both cases. These two expressions, occurring in parallel passages, explain one another; and further light is thrown on them by other passages in which the same words occur. It is thus clear that "in spirit" must be taken to mean "under the supernatural influence of God's Spirit," or, to put it in one word, "under Inspiration;" and that our Lord therefore recognises in the most distinct manner the Inspiration of at least some portion of the Old Testament.

6. This same Spirit whom Christ represents as animating the prophets of the Old Covenant, He promises to His Apostles to aid them in the preaching of the New. Thus in Matt. x. 19, He bids them "take no thought how or what you shall speak; for it shall be given you in that same hour what ye shall speak: for it is not ye

that speak, but the Spirit of your Father which speaketh in you;" or, as S. Luke has it, "For the Holy Ghost shall teach you in the same hour what ye ought to say." And in the last discourse recorded by S. John, a like assistance is promised, with the express object of enabling them to give to the world those truths which they had heard from their Master's lips: "The Comforter, which is the Holy Ghost, whom the Father will send in My name, He shall teach you all things, and bring all things to your remembrance, whatsoever I have said unto you;" "When the Comforter is come, He shall testify of Me; and ye also shall bear witness;" "When He, the Spirit of truth, is come, He will guide you into all truth, and He will show you things to come . . . He shall take of mine, and shall show it unto you[1]," (John xiv. 26, xv. 26, xvi. 12).

It is impossible, I think, to review these passages without feeling that the view of the Bible which our Lord impresses on us—the view which as man He Himself held—is substantially that which devout Christians have professed ever since,

---

[1] Although these promises allude primarily to preaching, we are fully warranted in extending them to the still more important matter of written teaching: see next page.

and profess still. To Him, as to them, it is the ultimate standard of appeal on matters of morality and conscience and truth; He silences temptation with the words "It is written," resting, not indeed on the letter, but on the spirit of God's ancient message to men. As an instrument of conversion He puts it in the very highest place. In one thrice-recorded passage He takes pains to assert that the Book of Exodus contains implicitly the supreme doctrine of a future life; and thereby He shows that not merely the direct statements, but also the deep allusions and obscure inferences of Scripture are to be sought out and accepted. Throughout, the Bible is treated as coming from God—as written by men under some higher and Divine influence, "in the Spirit," as He once says plainly—as having in it that supernatural element which it is the essence of the Natural theory to deny.

If Christ then has set the stamp of His authority upon the general contents of the Old Testament, may we extend the same witness to the New? It is clear that the passages quoted under head 6, fully warrant us in doing so. In Matt. x. 19 we have a special promise made for special circumstances. In the supreme hour of trial the Apostles need not perplex themselves in framing arguments or apologies; wisdom and eloquence would come of themselves, free gifts from God; nay it would not be themselves speaking, so much as God's Spirit speaking within them. Now, even if this passage stood alone, we might fairly infer that this Divine aid would not be absent on other occasions of equal moment, and especially in the composition of writings which were to transmit to all time the teachings of their Master. The passages in S. John however, as is often the case, give distinctly what the other Gospels only imply. The mysterious Paraclete—"the Comforter, which is the Holy Ghost"—was to be sent by the Father for this very end, that He might "teach the Apostles all things, and bring all things to their remembrance, whatsoever their Master had said to them." And why were these sayings to be recalled to their minds, but that they might transmit them to others, whether by word of mouth, or by writing? How can we wish a better warrant of Inspiration than is implied in the fact, that those who were to teach the world were themselves to be taught by the Holy Spirit of God?

We have seen what were our Lord's statements

with regard to the Inspiration of the Old Testament, and what were His promises with regard to that of the New. We naturally go on to enquire how these latter promises were fulfilled. Do the writings of the Apostles bear witness to the supernatural influence here foretold? Did the Paraclete really come to make His abode with them? And if so, what were the proofs of His coming, and the laws under which He acted upon their souls?

Our next work is therefore to trace the mission of the Spirit through the New Testament, and determine from the Apostles' own testimony what was its nature and extent.

"The Spirit of the Lord" is a term used occasionally throughout the Old Testament, but without being very clearly defined. It would be perhaps difficult to pronounce whether it implies a distinct Personality, or only as it were the personified energy of God. In the Synoptical Gospels there are many passages which, taken by themselves, would be of equally doubtful meaning. Such are Matt. xii. 18; xii. 28; Mark xii. 36; Luke i. 15; xi. 13. But there are others in which the Personality is much more clearly implied. John the Baptist sees the Spirit in a symbolic form descending on our Lord (Matt. iii. 16'; Mark i. 10): He Himself is led by the Spirit into the wilderness (Matt. iv. 1): blasphemy against the Holy Ghost is worse than blasphemy against the Son of Man (Matt. xii. 32): it is the Holy Ghost that speaks in the disciples (Mark xiii. 11), or teaches them (Luke xii. 12): Simeon has the approach of the Messiah revealed to him "by the Holy Ghost" (Luke ii. 26). But it is, as we might expect, in S. John's Gospel that the doctrine is brought into clearness and prominence, and this mainly by the words of Christ Himself. He first describes the Spirit, as the source of a new and inward life, in the remarkable conversation with Nicodemus (John iii). But this statement remains undeveloped till the time of His departure approaches, and His parting charge to His disciples begins. Then He promises (John xiv. 16) that to those who keep His commandments shall be given another Comforter, "that He may abide with you for ever, even the Spirit of Truth, whom the world cannot receive, because it seeth Him not, neither knoweth Him; but ye know Him; for He dwelleth with you, and shall be in you." This Comforter will teach them all things (xiv. 26), will testify of Christ (xv. 26), will convince the world of sin, of righteousness, and of judgment (xvi. 8), will guide into all truth (xvi. 13). All these promises, thus crowded together, must have produced on the Apostles' minds a very powerful impression, and prepared them for the scene in which their risen Lord (John xx. 22) solemnly bestowed on them the gift of the Holy Ghost. This bestowal, as we learn from St. Luke (Acts i. 5), was in the nature of ownership, not of immediate possession: the "baptism with the Holy Ghost," of which His forerunner had long ago spoken, should be accomplished on them "not many days hence;" and with these words almost on His lips the Master is parted from them and ascends to His Father's throne.

Such then was the promise of the Spirit: what do we read of its performance? On this head we have not far to seek. The Acts of the Apostles is full of the evidence which we require. It has been often observed what a marvellous change came over the disciples of Jesus of Nazareth immediately after He had been taken from them. Just when their cause might seem finally lost, and all their hopes blighted, they assumed as it were a new life and entered on a career of unheard-of success. The fearful grew courageous, the wavering steadfast, the unlearned became wise and eloquent. To what is this to be ascribed? That to which the disciples themselves ascribed it (as all who in any degree accept the Acts as authentic must admit) was none other than the power of the Holy Ghost. His influence is traced on every page. In the second chapter we read how He descended on the assembled Church; and the immediate effects are minutely described in the scene which follows. These were evidently accepted by the disciples as the fulfilment of the promise made to them by Christ; they were as evidently of a supernatural character, giving them not merely "a courage and wisdom which none of their adversaries were able to gainsay," but also such gifts as that of tongues, which, whatever signification we attach to it, was plainly superhuman. From thenceforward the allusions to the influence of the Spirit are frequent and regular. Peter is filled with the Holy Ghost, iv. 8; so are all the disciples, iv. 31. Ananias and his wife "lie to the Holy Ghost," and are supernaturally detected and punished, v. 4, 9. In v. 32 we find the Apostles saying of Christ, "We are His witnesses of these things, and so is also the Holy Ghost, whom God hath given to them that obey Him." The deacons are to be "men of honest report, full of the Holy Ghost and of wisdom," vi. 3; and we twice read of Stephen as being thus inspired, vi. 5 and vii. 55. By him we are told that the Israelites "resisted the Holy Ghost in the wilderness," vii. 51. The Apostles going down to Samaria pray for the new converts "that they might receive the Holy Ghost;" and by the laying on of their hands the Spirit is given, viii. 17. The effects are so clear and marvellous that Simon the magician would fain purchase with money so transcendant a gift, viii. 19. "An angel of the Lord" directs Philip on the road to Gaza, but the Spirit snatches him away when his errand is done, viii. 39. Saul is visited by Ananias, that he may receive his sight and "be filled with the Holy Ghost" ix. 17. The Churches "walk in the comfort of the Holy Ghost," ix. 31. The Spirit tells Peter how the men of Cornelius are seeking him, x. 19; and the Holy Ghost falls on Cornelius and his friends, x. 44. Barnabas is "full of the Holy Ghost and of faith," xi. 24; the Holy Ghost speaks through the prophets of Antioch, commanding to separate Barnabas and Saul, xiii. 2; Saul "filled with the Holy Ghost" withstands Elymas, xiii. 9; and in the same journey the disciples at Iconium are "filled with joy and with the Holy Ghost," xiii. 52. The Council of Jerusalem preface their decision with the remarkable words, "It seemed good to the Holy Ghost and to us," xv. 28. Paul is forbidden of the Holy Ghost to preach the word in Asia, and is not suffered to go into Bithynia, xvi. 7. At Ephesus the Holy Ghost comes on the disciples at the imposition of hands, and they speak with tongues and prophesy, xix. 6. At Miletus Paul testifies that "I go bound in the Spirit unto Jerusalem, not knowing the things that shall befall me there, save that the Holy Ghost witnesseth in every city, saying that bonds and afflictions abide me;" and at the same time he reminds the elders of Ephesus how the Holy Ghost had made them overseers over the flock, to feed the Church of God, xx. 28. At Tyre disciples say to Paul "through the Spirit" that he should not go up to Jerusalem, and Agabus (xxi. 11) prefaces a similar warning with the emphatic declaration of Inspiration, "Thus saith the Holy Ghost."

It is clear from these passages of the Acts that the Apostles believed themselves to be under the special direction of the Spirit in their preaching, their ordinances, their deliberations, and all the course of their ministry. In the Epistles indications of the same kind are found, though, as might be expected, much less frequently. But in 1 Cor. ii. 4 we find S. Paul saying, "My speech and my preaching was not with enticing words of man's wisdom, but in demonstration of the Spirit and of power;" and similarly (ii. 13), "which things also we speak, not in the words which man's wisdom teacheth, but which the Holy Ghost teacheth." In Col. i. 29 he describes himself as "striving according to His working, which worketh in me mightily;" and he reminds Titus (i. 3) how God "hath in due time manifested His word through preaching, which is committed unto me according to the commandment of God our Saviour." S. Peter also (1 Pet. i. 12) speaks of the things "which are now reported unto you by them that have preached the gospel unto you, with the Holy Ghost sent down from heaven;" and lastly, S. John prefaces the wonders of the Apocalypse by the statement that he "was in the Spirit on the Lord's day."

The chief passage in the Epistles upon this subject is however that contained in 1 Cor. xii–xiv. The manifold gifts of the Spirit are there discussed with a fulness which, though revealing much, leaves yet more involved in mystery to us, utterly without experience as we are of such phenomena. Into the exact nature of the various gifts of the Spirit, as described in this passage, there is no need for us to enter. That most of them were distinctly supernatural gifts is sufficiently proved by their names, "the word of wisdom," "the gifts of healing," "the working of miracles," "divers kinds of tongues," "the interpretation of tongues." They were evidently not universal, or necessarily permanent: yet so far constant that (as would appear from the very difficult allusions to the gift of tongues) they might at times be employed by the receiver at a time when they could edify none except himself. In that case however it was always possible to forego or defer their use (1 Cor. xiv. 27–30); they were thus under the control of the receiver's will, and tended always to edification, not to confusion.

It remains to show that this supernatural influence of the Spirit extended to the writings as well as to the other acts of the Apostles and their followers: in other words, that these writings are inspired, and were so regarded by their authors.

There are three lines of argument which unite to prove this fact, and each of which we will briefly consider. These are, (1) the *à priori* probability of the case; (2) the witness of the Apostles to the Inspiration of their own writings; (3) their witness to the Inspiration of the Old Testament, which implicitly proves to us that of the New Testament also, since no one at the present day will maintain the former to be inspired, and the latter not.

(1) If Inspiration was given to the Apostles in the delivery of oral discourses, the effect of which reached only to the few who formed the audience on each several occasion, it would be strange if it were absent in the composition of letters, which were to be read for the most part by a whole Church in the first instance, and were afterwards to be handed down through successive generations of believers to all future ages. If ever the Apostles might look with confidence for that Divine aid which had been promised, it would be in giving to the world the written message of their Lord. Thus, were there no direct evidence whatever on the point, we should properly conclude that the New Testament Scriptures were inspired, merely from the evidence already adduced as to the general Inspiration of the Apostles.

But (2) direct evidence on the point is by no means wanting. We may first point to the general style and tone of the Apostles' writings as proving clearly that they held themselves to be speaking with an authority other than their own. Thus S. Paul at the beginning of his letters is usually careful to call himself " an Apostle of Jesus Christ ;" with what object but to show that he claimed to speak, not in his own person, but as the ambassador and mouthpiece of his Lord? On special occasions he is doubly emphatic. Thus to the Galatians, who had gone astray after other teachers, he styles himself " Paul, an apostle not of man, neither by man, but by Jesus Christ, and God the Father who raised Him from the dead." And the Romans, to whom he was not as yet personally known, are addressed as from " Paul, a servant of Jesus Christ, called to be an apostle, separated unto the Gospel of God." The positive and fearless tone in which throughout his writings he lays down doctrines, decides questions, and reveals mysteries, could never have been endured for a moment if regarded as coming from a merely human teacher. Of all lines of evidence this, of general style and tenour, is perhaps the weightiest. But single passages of the most decisive character may also be adduced. S. Paul in putting before the Thessalonians the right view of the Resurrection day has this expression (1 Thess. iv. 15), "For this we say unto you *by the word of the Lord*[1], that we which are alive and remain" &c.; thus clearly calling in the weight of Divine authority to crush the human reasonings of his opponents. These same Thessalonians he enjoins in his Second Epistle (ii. 15) to "stand fast and hold the traditions which ye have been taught, whether by word or by our Epistle," a passage which in itself settles the question as to the spoken and written word standing on the same level of authority. It is moreover confirmed by two other verses in the same Epistle, ii. 2 and iii. 14. These admonitions are the more important when we consider that the Epistles to the Thessalonians are the earliest in date of all S. Paul's letters; and therefore in them we should naturally expect to find assertions of authority and inspiration which in later writings would be unnecessary, and therefore

---

[1] Ἐν λόγῳ Κυρίου. The preposition ἐν expresses more than is conveyed by the English "by." It shows that the word or "telling" of the Lord was infused into the message of the Apostle himself, or rather formed the sphere in which that message moved and had its being.

unexpressed. Singularly enough, the strongest of all other passages on Inspiration (from which in fact the name itself has doubtless arisen) comes from the very latest of all the Apostle's writings. This passage (which we propose further on to consider more fully) is in the Second Epistle to Timothy (iii. 14). Here S. Paul, speaking of the γραφαὶ of the Old Testament (a term which as will be shown is exactly equivalent to our word Scripture), says that they are "able to make wise unto salvation;" and then adds words which are translated (and I believe correctly translated) in our version as follows: "All Scripture is given by Inspiration of God, and is profitable for doctrine, for reproof, for correction, for instruction in righteousness." That this description of the Old Testament applies also to the New is proved (if it needs proof) by 1 Tim. v. 18, "For the Scripture saith, Thou shalt not muzzle the ox which treadeth out the corn; and, The labourer is worthy of his hire:" in which passage two citations, one from the Old Testament and one from the New (Luke x. 7), are alike comprehended[1] under the strictly technical

---

[1] This is the simple and natural sense of the passage, whatever may be said against it.

THE NATURAL THEORY. 31

term of $\gamma\rho\alpha\phi\dot{\eta}$. So too S. Peter (2 Pet. iii. 2) in one breath enjoins his hearers to be "mindful of the words which were spoken before by the holy prophets, and of the commandments of us, the Apostles of the Lord and Saviour." Lastly, this same Apostle may be said to clinch our argument in one striking passage (2 Pet. iii. 15), in which the letters of his "brother Paul" (whom the vanity of modern criticism would represent as his lifelong antagonist) are classed indiscriminately with the inspired canon, "in which are some things hard to be understood, which they that are unlearned and unstable wrest, as they do also the other scriptures, to their own destruction."

(3) We have just shown that the Apostles placed their own writings and those of the Old Testament on the same footing. But it may be asked in what light did they regard the latter? The answer to this question forms the third branch of evidence as to the Apostolic views upon Inspiration. It may be said generally that they cite it and appeal to it in exactly the same way, and with just the same reverence and confidence, as is usual amongst Christians of the present day. In one word, they hold it, as we do, to be the Word of God. The passages which

establish this conclusion are numerous, and may be classed under the following heads:—

(*a*) The strongest passages are perhaps those which quote words of the Old Testament as actually spoken or delivered by God, the writers being only mentioned, if at all, as the channel through which they are transmitted to us. A typical passage is that which occurs in the very first chapter of the New Testament, Matt. i. 22, "Now all this was done that it might be fulfilled which was spoken of the Lord by the prophet, saying," &c. (ὑπὸ τοῦ Κυρίου διὰ τοῦ προφήτου); where the Greek prepositions accurately define the source and the channel of the inspired saying. Again, in Acts i. 16 we have the same fact expressed in different but still plainer language, and that in the report of a speech by S. Peter himself, the first of the Apostles: "This Scripture must needs have been fulfilled, which the Holy Ghost by the mouth of David spake before concerning Judas." A little later in the history (Acts iii. 21) the same Apostle speaks of "the times of restitution of all things, which God hath spoken by the mouth of all His holy prophets since the world began." In the same book are found similar passages, iv. 25, xiii. 34, xxviii. 25,

THE NATURAL THEORY. 33

the last confirming by the mouth of S. Paul what we have already had on the authority of S. Peter: "Well spake the Holy Ghost by Esaias the prophet unto our fathers, saying," &c. Passages of almost equal strength are easily to be found in the Epistles; see Rom. i. 1, iii. 2 (in which the title of "the oracles of God" is applied to the Scriptures), ix. 25, 1 Cor. xv. 27[1], 2 Cor. vi. 16, 1 Tim. iv. 1; and especially the Epistle to the Hebrews, which is remarkable for the number of passages in which it quotes language of the Old Testament as spoken by God or by the Holy Ghost: see Heb. i. 1, i. 6, ii. 11, iii. 7 ("Wherefore as the Holy Ghost saith, To-day if ye will hear His voice"), iv. 4, v. 5, viii. 7, ix. 8, x. 5, x. 15, x. 30, xii. 26, xiii. 5. Lastly, we have two remarkable passages of S. Peter, which, being crucial passages as regards Inspiration, will hereafter receive a fuller discussion. At present we need only quote 1 Peter i. 11 "searching what or what manner of time the Spirit of Christ which was in them did testify;"

---

[1] That God, not the Scripture, is the understood subject in this passage (ὅταν δὲ εἴπῃ ὅτι πάντα ὑποτέτακται) is clear from the use of the word εἴπῃ instead of λέγῃ, the latter word being always used whenever the Scripture is described as saying anything.

and 2 Peter i. 21, "holy men of old spake as they were moved by the Holy Ghost."

(*b*) There are other passages in which words from the Old Testament are cited, not indeed as having been spoken by God, but at the same time as being true prophecy—prophecy which would receive, and as it were demanded fulfilment. A striking instance of this is found, in John xix. 28, "After this, Jesus knowing that all things were now accomplished, that the Scripture might be fulfilled, saith, I thirst." Even if we should take the ἵνα in this passage as equivalent to "so that," and indicating consequence only, it would show that, to the mind of S. John, the fulfilment of Scripture was a thing to be looked for and recorded even at that last tremendous moment of his Master's life. But there are at least some grounds for assuming far more than this. The word rendered "fulfilled" is not πληρόω (the regular term used for the fulfilment of Scripture, and so found only a few verses back, xix. 24), but τελειόω, "to make perfect," "to complete," the word which our Lord uses when He says (John xvii. 4), "I have finished the work which Thou gavest Me to do." Moreover Christ is the subject of the sentence, and in it we are told that at that moment He knew or saw that all things (all things, that is, relating to His Incarnation and Passion) were now accomplished, brought to an end (τετέλεσται, a cognate word to τελειόω). Does it not then seem probable that the two clauses should be connected together; and that the word "that" (ἵνα) must express the purpose with which our Lord gave utterance to that one token of bodily anguish, namely, lest one jot or tittle of the inspired predictions should in the last moment pass unfulfilled? If such be the Apostle's meaning, it is impossible to conceive a more emphatic testimony to the authority and importance which must, in the eyes of Christ, have belonged to the Scriptures of the Old Testament.

Of a similar character to the above passage are those in which some event is said to have happened in order that some prophecy might be fulfilled, or, in other words, that God's counsel, already declared in Holy Scripture, might be at length realised in action. Thus S. Matthew (iv. 14) says that our Lord came and dwelt in Capernaum "that it might be fulfilled which was spoken by Esaias the prophet, saying, The land of Zabulon and the land of Nephthalim," &c. He uses similar expressions in other passages, viii. 17,

xiii. 35, xxi. 4, xxvii. 9. S. Mark, writing presumably for Romans, does not thus quote Jewish prophecy, the only apparent exception, xv. 28, being probably an interpolation. In S. Luke again such references are wanting; but they return in S. John, once in chap. xii. 14, "As it is written, Fear not, daughter of Zion," &c.; and three times in chap. xix, one of these being the passage already cited, and the other two being ver. 24 ("that the Scripture might be fulfilled which saith, They parted My raiment among them," &c.); and ver. 36 ("For these things were done that the Scripture should be fulfilled, A bone of Him shall not be broken.")

Again, in the second chapter of Acts, S. Peter, speaking as a Jew to Jews, appeals four several times to the Scriptures they alike acknowledged (vv. 16, 25, 30, 34); and we find the same in other speeches, as iv. 11, xv. 15. Nor does S. Paul fail to afford the like testimony: see the repeated quotations from the Old Testament in the ninth chapter of Romans (vv. 13, 25, 27, 29, 33); also 1 Cor. xv. 54, Gal. iii. 8, of which the latter is very remarkable from the bold personification of Scripture which is employed—"The Scripture, foreseeing that God would justify the heathen through faith, preached before the Gospel unto Abraham, saying," &c. Lastly, the same habit of quotation is found in the Epistle to the Hebrews (ii. 6), and that of S. James (ii. 23).

(*c*) Statements of the Old Testament are quoted by the Apostles as literally and historically true, although of a supernatural character. Such passages are 1 Cor. xv. 45, "And so it is written, The first man Adam was made a living soul;" and 2 Cor. xi. 3, "Lest by any means, as the serpent beguiled Eve through his subtilty, so your minds should be corrupted," &c. In other cases the fact quoted is a special revelation of God to man: see Rom. ix. 15, "For He saith to Moses, I will have mercy on whom I will have mercy" (a citation from that most remarkable history of the proclamation of the name of the Lord in Exodus chap. xxxiii); also Rom. xi. 2, Acts iii. 21–25.

(*d*) The Old Testament is cited as the supreme authority and last appeal on matters of doctrine —a position it can only hold as being an express revelation from God. As we might expect it is S. Paul who furnishes us with this head of evidence; thus in Rom. i. 17, when beginning to open out his view of justification, he confirms it by a quotation from Habakkuk; "as it is written,

The just shall live by faith." Further on (iv. 3) he makes a weapon for himself out of another passage, "For what saith the Scripture? Abraham believed God, and it was counted unto him for righteousness." See also in the same Epistle, iii. 10, iv. 7, iv. 17, x. 5. In Galatians (iii. 10–13) where he is in like manner contrasting the righteousness of the law with that of faith, we have three such citations close together; lastly, in Ephesians (iv. 8) he regards the effects of Christ's ascension into heaven as having been foreshadowed in one of the noblest of sacred poems, the sixty-eighth Psalm.

(*e*) The Old Testament is further appealed to as a guide and authority in spiritual matters generally, much as the Bible is appealed to by religious writers now. Here again the chief examples come from the Epistles of S. Paul. Thus we have in Rom. x. 11, "For the Scripture saith, Whosoever believeth on Him shall not be ashamed." Rom. x. 15, "How shall they preach except they be sent? as it is written, How beautiful are the feet of them that preach the gospel of peace and bring glad tidings of good things." See also Rom. xiv. 11, xv. 3, 1 Cor. i. 19 ("For it is written, I will destroy the wisdom of the wise," &c.), i. 31, iii. 19, xiv. 21, Eph. vi. 2 ("Honour thy father and thy mother; which is the first commandment with promise,") 1 Tim. v. 18, James ii. 8 ("If ye fulfil the royal law according to the Scripture, Thou shalt love thy neighbour as thyself, ye do well,") James iv. 5, 1 Pet. i. 16.

Akin to these are the references to the figurative or allegorical meanings of Scripture. There is a tendency in modern times to deny the existence of such meanings altogether; but they are clearly recognised by the Apostles; witness the singular passage in Galatians, iv. 21-30, in which S. Paul applies to the earthly and heavenly Jerusalem the apparently matter-of-fact history of Hagar and Sarah: or again, the reference by S. Peter (1 Peter ii. 6) to the Corner Stone as being typical of Christ, an application which had already been made by our Lord Himself in His repeated quotations from the 118th Psalm.

(*f*) Lastly, there are two passages in which the Law is spoken of as given not directly by God, but through the mediation of angels, viz. Gal. iii. 19 ("It was ordained by angels in the hand of a mediator,") and Hebrews ii. 2 ("If the word spoken by angels was stedfast). Whatever may be the exact meaning to be attached to these expressions, it is clear that they claim for the Old Testament a distinctly supernatural origin.

We will now recapitulate briefly the evidence that has been brought forward in this first branch of our investigation.

First, we have the witness of Christ Himself. He quotes the Old Testament as containing true prophecies both as to Himself and as to others, prophecies which would be certainly and accurately fulfilled,—as a treasury of moral and spiritual truth from which lessons of belief and conduct might unerringly be drawn,—as having even in minute phrases a depth and fulness of meaning which altogether transcends any human power of composition,—as forming a persuasive to repentance which will succeed, wherever success is possible. He also speaks of David as being specially inspired by the Holy Spirit in the composition of the 116th Psalm; and this same Holy Spirit He promises in set terms shall descend on His Apostles after His own departure, and aid them by supernatural ways in the preaching of the new faith.

THE NATURAL THEORY. 41

Next we show that the Spirit did in truth come to do His predicted work. This is abundantly proved from the Acts of the Apostles. It is clear that to the writer of that book the existence and operation of the Spirit was a proved and palpable fact, confirmed in innumerable instances. The personages of the narrative are continually giving or receiving the "gift of the Holy Ghost;" continually enjoying the comfort, following the direction, or heeding the warnings of the Spirit. The same appears from various passages of the Epistles, especially the long discourse on "spiritual gifts" contained in 1 Cor. xii–xiv. It remains to show that this supernatural assistance extended to the writings as well as to the oral teaching of apostolic men. This is established by three lines of argument. (1) the intrinsic probability of the case; (2) the direct evidence of several passages; (3) the way in which the writers of the New Testament quote and make use of the Old Testament, which is identical with that already sanctioned by our Lord and subsequently adopted by Christians of all ages, and which fully recognises the truth and divine Inspiration of those writings. This implicitly goes to prove the Inspiration of the New

Testament also, as no one will now assert that the former is inspired and the latter not.

If then the Bible is to be credited at all—if it is in any sense the work of honest and intelligent men—then it appears that we must accept it on its own authority as being in deed and in truth the Word of God; as not merely containing the record, more or less exact, of a revelation once given to men of old, but as being itself in form and substance an actual written Revelation to us. The divine element in it is therefore immeasurably greater than would be ascribed to it by the natural theory; and this theory is therefore discovered to fall very far short of the truth.

This then would seem to be the result of an examination not of isolated passages but of the general tenour and teaching of the New Testament. The test, it is to be observed, is altogether an indirect one. In the texts quoted the writers were not thinking about Inspiration in itself, or giving their views upon it. All we have done is to judge by the tenour of their language what their convictions on the subject must have been. In this, as in so many other cases, the teaching of the Bible is implicit rather than explicit. But are there then no passages whatever which bear directly on the subject; none in which the Apostles actually set themselves to tell us something about that Inspiration the existence of which they clearly recognise both with regard to themselves and to the authors of the older canon? To this it must be answered that there are passages of this kind which, though not numerous, are of the highest importance. These special passages on Inspiration (as they may be termed) we shall now proceed to examine; and we shall show that they strongly confirm the indirect evidence which we have already brought forward.

First special passage on Inspiration, 1 Cor. ii. 12, 13. "Now we have received not the spirit of the world, but the spirit which is of God; that we might know the things that are freely given unto us of God. Which things also we speak, not in the words which man's wisdom teacheth, but which the Holy Ghost teacheth; comparing spiritual things with spiritual."

We must first observe that the direct reference here is to oral teaching—" which things we speak (λαλοῦμεν):" and the tenour of the whole passage shows that S. Paul has specially in his mind his preaching to the Corinthians at his first visit amongst them (see ii. 1, ii. 4, iii. 1). But we have already shown that any information given as to the inspiration of the Apostles' spoken discourses may undoubtedly, and almost *à fortiori*, be extended to their written ones. Nay, this passage is itself a corroboration of this statement; for it is impossible to believe that S. Paul would have disclaimed for the solemn words here written to his converts that high authority and inspiration, which he is expressly claiming for the words spoken to those same converts in time past. Hence we may take the words as indicating the light in which S. Paul viewed his own teaching, whether by letter or by word of mouth.

What then does the Apostle say? At the beginning of his letter he has been deprecating the party spirit which was springing up in the Corinthian Church—the disposition to attach themselves to one teacher or to another, to give their faith to Paul or Apollos or Cephas, and not to the common doctrine which they taught. In strenuous opposition to this tendency, it is his aim to contrast the dignity, the power of the one message with the feebleness and insignificance of the many messengers. The preaching of the

Cross is indeed foolishness in the eyes of the world, but it is a foolishness of God which is wiser than man's wisdom, stronger than man's strength. Nay, it comes expressly to supersede that wisdom by which the world "knew not God;" and therefore it keeps altogether clear of those "enticing words," that "excellency of speech" by which the philosophers and sages strove to recommend their theories. Of this, he takes pains to remind them, he himself is an example; when he came among them at the first, it was not "with excellency of speech or of wisdom," but rather "in weakness and in fear and in much trembling." So coming he preached however; and in his preaching there was nothing to to be noted of feebleness or of fear. It was delivered "in demonstration of the Spirit—$\dot{\epsilon}\nu$ $\dot{a}\pi o\delta\epsilon i\xi\epsilon\iota$ $\Pi\nu\epsilon\acute{\upsilon}\mu a\tau o\varsigma$:" it was "the power of God;" it was "wisdom to those that are perfect—the hidden wisdom—the wisdom of God in a mystery." The world knows nothing of it, but to him and his fellow-workers it is known: and wherefore? Because "God hath revealed it by His Spirit;" because "we have received not the spirit of the world, but the Spirit which is of God, that we might know the things that are freely given to us of God."

In such repeated phrases he dwells on the fact that in his teaching there is a truly Divine element, springing from that Spirit of God which abides in him, and which searches the deep things of God to reveal them to him. Nor does this influence extend only to the substance, the general scope of his preaching; in verse 13 we have the assurance that the very words he uses are not without their inspiration; "which things we speak, not in the words which man's wisdom teacheth, but which the Holy Ghost teacheth, comparing spiritual things with spiritual," or rather perhaps, " using a spiritual standard for spiritual things."

For our present purpose it is sufficient to note that, far from regarding his own discourses as a mere product of human intellect (which would be the case according to the natural theory), S. Paul draws the sharpest possible contrast between the two. Nothing can be clearer than that he regards himself and his fellow labourers as speaking under an immediate and supernatural revelation from God, given "by His Spirit." If therefore we embrace the natural theory, we must hold either that S. Paul and his friends were the victims of an[1] unheard of delusion, or that he was designedly

---

[1] It may of course be said that there have been at various

saying what he knew to be false. To those then who accept the New Testament as true, this passage in itself forms a proof that the natural theory is not a complete account of Inspiration. The light which it throws upon the literal theory will be discussed further on.

Second special passage on Inspiration, 2 Tim. iii. 14-17. " But continue thou in the things which thou hast learned and hast been assured of, knowing of whom thou hast learned them; and that from a child thou hast known the holy Scriptures, which are able to make thee wise unto salvation through faith which is in Christ Jesus. All Scripture is given by inspiration of God, and is profitable for doctrine, for reproof, for correction, for instruction in righteousness: that the man of God may be perfect, throughly furnished unto all good works."

times many who have professed themselves inspired by the Holy Spirit to promulgate the wildest notions. But it is to be observed (1) that it is very doubtful whether all of these persons may not be classed either as deliberate impostors, or as distinctly insane; (2) that ravings of this kind have one universal characteristic—*they are not original;* they are imitations, caricatures of something their authors have found elsewhere, generally in the Bible itself. But of S. Paul's teaching the prototype can be found nowhere; neither in the prophecies of the Old Testament, nor the discourses of Christ, nor the philosophy of Greece, nor the mysticism of Alexandria; whatever else we may think of it, it is his own.

Of all New Testament passages bearing on our subject this is perhaps the most striking; the word Inspiration is found here and here only, as is the Greek (θεόπνευστος) of which it is the equivalent. As, however, the true sense of the clause containing this word has been much disputed, we may make this observation at the outset. Whatever the clause be taken to mean, it at least asserts this: that there is such a thing as Scripture which is inspired, or to translate literally, "God-breathed," a term of which the strength and vividness may be left to speak for themselves; and that this Scripture is of use for instructing, for convincing, for restoring, (literally, "setting upright again,") and generally for education in righteousness. It is difficult to conceive what more could be said on behalf of the Bible.

Let us now endeavour to discover the real and exact meaning of the words here used as to Inspiration (πᾶσα γραφὴ θεόπνευστος καὶ ὠφέλιμος, &c.) There are only two probable translations; one is substantially that of our version, and the other (which at the present day is probably the most in favour) will run thus, "All inspired Scripture is also profitable," &c. According to the first rendering "inspired" and "profitable," are both predicates, giving different characteristics of Scripture; according to the second, "profitable" is the only predicate, and "inspired" is merely an epithet. There is good authority for both translations. In support of the authorized version Bishop Middleton (On the Greek Article, p. 391) remarks that he knows no instance of so violent a disjunction of two adjectives apparently united by a copula. On the other hand, Bishop Ellicott and Dr. Donaldson prefer the second rendering, for reasons which will be discussed further on. Bishop Wordsworth, in his Notes on the New Testament, insists on a third meaning, which was first given by Origen, and is that of the Syriac and other [1] versions. According to this, θεόπνευστος forms a clause in itself, giving the reason why Scripture is profitable, namely, that it is inspired; and the translation will be, "All Scripture, being inspired" (or "inasmuch as it is inspired") "is also profitable," &c. But were this the meaning, surely we should find οὖσα or γενομένη with θεόπνευστος. A clause thus formed of an adjective alone without a participle would be extremely harsh in

---

[1] He also quotes the Vulgate in its favour: "Omnis Scriptura divinitus inspirata utilis est." But it is clear that these words would equally suit the second rendering.

classical Greek, and is I believe quite unknown in the New Testament.

We have then to choose between the first and second renderings. It may, I think, be admitted that were the passage found in a classical author, the second translation would be the accepted and correct one; though even there some allowance should be made for the fact that scholars are usually prejudiced in favour of the more idiomatic and difficult construction. But the Greek of the New Testament has its own laws; and I shall endeavour to show (so far as the scope of this work will allow) that the first translation (that of the Authorized Version) gives the true meaning of the present passage.

We should first observe that nothing certain can be concluded from the analogy of similar passages, for the reason that these scarcely exist. An exactly similar construction is only found once in the New Testament, viz. 1 Tim. iv. 4, Πᾶν κτίσμα Θεοῦ καλὸν καὶ οὐδὲν ἀπόβλητον " every creature of God is good, and nothing to be refused." The sense here is clearly according to our first translation; and as this passage also comes from the Pastoral Epistles, it carries much weight. But whilst usage is thus

THE NATURAL THEORY. 51

in favour of the first interpretation, it cannot be considered as conclusive on the matter.

But the true argument is drawn from the meaning of the words involved. Our second translation ran, "All inspired Scripture is profitable." This has a strange sound to modern English ears; for to those who have been taught that the whole of Scripture is inspired, and that other writings are not, the epithet seems as superfluous as if we were to hear of " all luminous stars." If, on the other hand, we could translate, " Every inspired writing," the epithet would seem natural and needful, as marking off that class of writings the utility of which is to be insisted on. But so to translate is impossible.

From a careful examination of the numerous passages in which the word γραφὴ occurs, it will appear that the word[1] (originally meaning "writing" in general) is restricted by the authors of the New Testament to the writings of the sacred canon, thus exactly resembling the English

---

[1] The word used in the New Testament for writings in general is γράμματα. See John v. 47 (where it is contrasted with ῥήματα); Luke xvi. 6; John vii. 15 (πῶς οὗτος γράμματα οἶδε); Acts xxvi. 24; xxviii. 21. The one case where this is used of the Scriptures is in the present passage (2 Tim. iii. 15), but here it is carefully qualified by the epithet ἱερὰ ("the sacred writings").

correlative "Scripture." The meanings which it assumes are as follows:—

1. γραφή is used for a particular passage or text of the Bible, e.g. Mark xv. 28, καὶ ἐπληρώθη ἡ γραφὴ ἡ λέγουσα, &c. Similar expressions are frequent in S. John, as xix. 36, "that the Scripture might be fulfilled, A bone of Him shall not be broken: and again another Scripture saith, They shall look on Him whom they pierced;" compare in the same chapter verses 24, 28, also xiii. 18, xx. 9.

2. ἡ γραφή is used for the book as a whole, often in a sort of personification, just as we use 'Scripture" or "the Bible:" thus John vii. 42, οὐχὶ ἡ γραφὴ εἶπεν ὅτι ἐκ τοῦ σπέρματος Δαυίδ, &c. This is especially the use in the Epistles, as Rom. iv. 3, τί γὰρ ἡ γραφὴ λέγει; Rom. ix. 17, λέγει γὰρ ἡ γραφὴ τῷ Φαραώ: also x. 11, xi. 2, Gal. iii. 8, iii. 22, &c. There are cases (as Rom. x. 11) where it may be a question whether this or No. 2 is the true sense of the passage. To this sense belongs a remarkable passage of S. Peter (2 Peter i. 20), which will be fully considered lower down. This, however, is the place to remark that πᾶσα προφητεία γραφῆς cannot mean anything but "every prophecy of Scripture," or more shortly, "every Scripture prophecy." No passage can show more

clearly that γραφή was applied to the writings of the Bible only.

3. In a few passages αἱ γραφαὶ in the plural is used, not collectively of the Scripture writings as a whole (as in 1), but severally, as expressing the different portions and books of which it is made up. These are the only places in which it could possibly be suggested that the word was used in a general sense as a "writing;" but a glance at them will show that such a suggestion is untenable. They are as follows:—(i) Matt. xxvi. 56, ἵνα πληρωθῶσιν αἱ γραφαὶ τῶν προφητῶν. Here the distinction is between other parts of the Old Testament and the prophetical books, so that the words are rightly translated "the Scriptures of the prophets." (ii) Luke xxiv. 27, διηρμήνευεν αὐτοῖς ἐν πάσαις ταῖς γραφαῖς. This passage in itself proves that γραφαὶ means "Scriptures" only, and not "writings" in general, since it clearly refers to the former only, and yet speaks of πᾶσαι γραφαί. (iii) Rom. i. 2, ὃ προεπηγγείλατο διὰ τῶν προφητῶν αὐτοῦ ἐν γραφαῖς ἁγίαις. Here, by Bishop Middleton's well-known rule, the words following the preposition should be translated as if they had the article; the rendering will therefore be, "by his prophets in the holy Scriptures," ἅγιος being

used here as an epithet of veneration only, as it is continually in the expression τὸ ἅγιον Πνεῦμα. (iv) Rom. xvi. 26, διά τε γραφῶν προφητικῶν ... γνωρισθέντος. To this might be applied the same remarks as to the last example; but another explanation is possible. For these γραφαὶ προφητικαὶ are said to be the means used for making known to all the Gentiles the mystery long concealed, but now made manifest; and as this does not apply to the Old Testament Scriptures, it seems probable that S. Paul is really alluding to the Scriptures of the New Testament, which, as they were written by himself and his fellow-labourers, were continually being spread through the countries of the world. In this case the absence of the article is to be expected, because the canon was not yet complete, and it was not therefore as yet possible to speak of "*the* prophetic Scriptures." This interpretation is supported by our last example. (v) 2 Pet. iii. 16, στρεβλοῦσιν, ὡς καὶ τὰς λοιπὰς γραφάς. S. Peter is here speaking of the epistles of S. Paul, and this passage therefore establishes two facts: (*a*) that those epistles had already received the sacred title of γραφή; (*b*) that this title is restricted to the inspired writings alone, since otherwise τὰς λοιπὰς γραφὰς would include the whole of literature.

If then γραφή is the exact equivalent of "Scripture," what will be the force of the expression πᾶσα γραφή? To ascertain this we must examine the passages in which πᾶς occurs without the article. It will be found to have the following three meanings:—

(i.) Used *severally*, corresponding to the English "every." Of this a well-known example is the metrical line (James i. 17), πᾶσα δόσις ἀγαθὴ καὶ πᾶν δώρημα τέλειον, "every good gift, and every perfect gift:" other examples exist, as Jas. iii. 7, but they are few in number.

(ii.) Used *collectively*, corresponding to the English "all" with a collective noun: as in John xvii. 1, ἐξουσίαν πάσης σαρκὸς, "power over all flesh;" Rev. viii. 7, πᾶς χόρτος χλωρός, "all green grass."

(iii.) Used to signify *completeness*, corresponding to the English "all" in such phrases as "all praise, all glory, honour, power;" this usage is by no means uncommon, as in 1 Tim. iv. 9, πάσης ἀποδοχῆς ἄξιος, "worthy of all acceptation."

It is clear that this last sense does not apply to our present passage, and that our choice must lie between (i) and (ii). If we choose the first, and assume that the three words πᾶσα γραφὴ θεόπνευστος must be taken together, we can only translate "every inspired writing;" if the second, we may render "all inspired Scripture." But the first translation is rendered impossible by the proof just given, that γραφή never means writing in general, but always the sacred Scripture in particular. We are then thrown back upon the second translation. In that case there seem only two possible interpretations of the clause: (1) that S. Paul wishes to divide the Scriptures into two classes, inspired and non-inspired, and to claim for one what he disclaims for the other; (2) that the word θεόπνευστος is a mere redundant epithet, applied by way of respect, as we often use "holy" of the Bible in English. Now the distinction implied in (1) is one of which we have absolutely no hint whatever in any other passage of the Bible. It is completely opposed to the spirit and tenour of all references to Scripture made either by Christ or His Apostles, as may be seen from the exposition given above. To import it here into a single disputed passage is therefore utterly inadmissible. As to (2) we may remark that if there is one point of expression more foreign than another to the quick, passionate, incisive style of S. Paul's letters, it is a use of redundant epithets. Moreover, out of forty-four cases in which γραφή is found in the New Testament, there is but one other where it is used with anything that can be construed into a mere epithet of respect, viz. Rom. i. 2, ἐν γραφαῖς ἁγίαις. Lastly, had there been no thought in S. Paul's mind beyond a momentary expression of reverence for the writings he was commending, it is almost impossible that he could have used such an epithet as θεόπνευστος— a word which, so far as I know, is unknown to literature before or since[1], being coined by the writer for this occasion, and this occasion only, and a word which is of such singular depth and force that it may well be said to contain implicitly all which it is the aim of this essay to elucidate. I believe it will be felt on thoughtful consideration that this really forms one of the strongest arguments for the word being taken as a predicate, not as an epithet. Whatever the degree of force we may attach to this however, I think it is clear that neither the first nor the second interpretations of the clause, as stated above, can possibly be admitted; and since, if we take θεόπνευστος as an epithet, we are compelled to adopt one or other

---

[1] The word is unknown to classical Greek, but is of course formed on the analogy of such words as θεόδμητος (Homer and Pindar); θεόληπτος = "inspired" (Plutarch); θεόρρητος (Anthology), and others.

of these, it seems to be established that the word is really a predicate, and that the translation of the Authorized Version is correct. What S. Paul was here aiming at, therefore, was to impress deeply on his disciple's mind, in this last message of love, that those Scriptures, which he left to him as his guide to wisdom, were more, much more, than a mere human production; that they were (and here we may conceive him pausing to search for, and finally to construct, a word which should fully express his meaning,) "God-breathed,"—a word which brings out sharp and clear those two elements in Scripture of which I have treated from the commencement: since it must imply both a power that breathes, and also a vessel that is breathed into; a body which is human, a Spirit which is divine. I have used this last word advisedly, because I cannot doubt that one analogy was present to S. Paul's mind, which no English rendering can well transmit; that in using the term πνεῦστος he was not without a thought of that Πνεῦμα on whose influences he loved to dwell; that the Breather implied a breath, and that this breath was itself in this case a Person and Divine.

It must therefore be acknowledged, I believe, that this passage is of very great and peculiar import; expressing the solemn and deliberate judgment of S. Paul, in the very last days of his life, as to the inspiration and the value of that book, which through the whole of that life had been his study and his guide. Any man who will well consider what such a judgment of S. Paul's must mean, may also be content to rest his belief in Inspiration on this sentence alone.

The other special passages we have to discuss will not detain us so long; they are as follows:—

1 Pet. i. 10–12, "Of which salvation the prophets have enquired and searched diligently, who prophesied of the grace that should come unto you: searching what, or what manner of time the Spirit of Christ which was in them did signify, when it testified beforehand the sufferings of Christ, and the glory that should follow. Unto whom it was revealed, that not unto us they did minister the things which are now reported unto you by them that have preached the Gospel unto you with the Holy Ghost sent down from heaven."

The first point which strikes us here is the unusual phrase πνεῦμα Χρίστου[1], "the Spirit of

---

[1] There is some authority for reading πνεῦμα Θεοῦ here; but this is just a case where the more rare and difficult reading is to be preferred.

Christ;" which is only found in one other passage, Rom. viii. 9, " If any man have not the Spirit of Christ, he is none of His," (εἴ τις πνεῦμα Χρίστου οὐκ ἔχει οὗτος οὐκ ἔστιν αὐτοῦ). It there appears as a significant variant of the expression several times appearing in the context, "the Spirit of God," (πνεῦμα Θεοῦ). And the motive of the use seems to be the same in both passages, viz. to draw attention to the intimate union existing between the three Persons of the Trinity. In the chapter now before us it is especially appropriate. S. Peter has been exhorting his flock to live rejoicing in the salvation that has come to them; and that in spite of manifold trials wherewith for the moment they may be oppressed. And, like a wise teacher, he does not seek to encourage them by making light of their sufferings, or by depicting the greater miseries of himself or of others; but bids them see in these troubles one act of a long and glorious drama—a drama in which all good men play heroic parts, under Christ, the great Protagonist; a drama to which prophets of old looked forward with eager interest, striving as it were to lift the veil of the future, to realize what was meant by those dim but glorious presages, which they flung ever and anon upon the stream of the ages, not knowing what they spake, moved by a power which was not theirs, but which they felt and knew to be the Spirit of God. And not only was he the Spirit of God (so the Apostle would seem so say), but also the Spirit of Him, whose sufferings and whose humiliation formed the mysterious burden of those prophecies. Christ has always been with His own; He was with them in early days when His own life on earth was only a foreshadowed mystery: He was with them when it became a present reality: He is with them now, when it is a memory and a possession for ever. Those faithful few to whom the Apostle writes are partakers with Christ in the sufferings that precede: they will also be partakers in the glories that follow. If this be the dominant idea of the chapter, we can see, I think, why S. Peter in speaking of the Spirit is fain to call Him the Spirit of Christ; and why he also brings in that striking picture of the old prophets looking onwards, in dim faith, to that great spectacle which Christian men were now offering in its reality to men and to angels. It is this picture however which is at the moment our chief concern. It lets us, as perhaps no other passage does, into the secret of a prophet's consciousness; it shows us a divinely-gifted man foretelling a dispensation of grace to be realized in a far distant future; feeling that a Spirit was in him which was not his own spirit, but rather the Spirit of God: describing, under the influence of that Spirit, the sufferings and the conquests of the Messiah, but without any knowledge of the time or conjuncture, near or far, at which they were to take place; longing and striving in vain to discern this for himself; receiving at length a further Revelation, that it was not to his own times, but to a far-distant generation, that his words applied; a generation to whom (as the Apostle concludes) that great life and death were being taught as an accomplished fact, by the lips of men not less truly inspired by that same heaven-sent Spirit (ἐν Πνεύματι ἁγίῳ) than were those old prophets themselves. We have thus an intimation, not less distinct and weighty because indirect, that the prophecies of the Old Testament were spoken under a divine inspiration, and that the same influence was present to the authors of the New.

The one remaining passage to be examined is from the same writer as the last, and is as follows:—

2 Pet. i. 19 sqq., "We have also a more sure

word of prophecy; whereunto ye do well that ye take heed, as unto a light that shineth in a dark place, until the day dawn, and the day star arise in your hearts: knowing this first, that no prophecy of the Scripture is of any private interpretation. For the prophecy came not in old time by the will of man: but holy men of God spake as they were moved by the Holy Ghost."

Although the motive of this passage is in some respects similar to that we have last considered, yet it differs widely in this, that whereas in the first S. Peter was looking outwards to his flock and thinking only of them, their trials and their hopes, in the second he is looking inwards upon himself, reviewing calmly and for the last time the evidences on which his life's work has rested as its foundation. True, he has in the first part of the chapter exhorted his hearers to lengthen and complete their roll of virtues, to use all diligence to make their calling and election sure; and thus to secure their entrance into the invisible and eternal kingdom of Christ. But he goes on to apologize, as it were, for this urgency, by telling them that this was the last appeal of one about to pass away, and zealous that his teaching should not pass away also. And here he seems as it were to pause, and, with death just before him, turn round once more and look back to see what that teaching had been, and whereon it had rested. They were not, he says, "cunningly devised fables," cobwebs spun by the brains of sophists, on which his lifelong preachings were based; but rather they stood secure on two broad and deep foundations—on the one side weighty facts of Christ's majesty and power, which his own eyes had seen and his own ears had heard—or the other[1] a foundation yet more secure and steadfast (if such indeed could be), namely, the "prophetic word," the great message of Scripture, which shone for them as a lamp in a dark place, until the day broke, and the morning star rose above the horizon of their hearts. And then, as to the right appreciation of this light, he gives them a special caution, which is contained in verses 20, 21, and which concerns us now beyond the rest of the passage. For Scripture, as he has said, is a lamp only in the darkness, sufficient to guide

[1] It seems probable that at this point S. Peter was not thinking of himself (for what could be more certain than the evidence of his own senses?) but of his hearers, to whom the whole chain of prophecy offered a more overwhelming array of evidence than the testimony, however cogent, of any single man.

but not to illuminate—that must be left till the dawn of another day. And for this purpose of guidance it must be used aright, and with strict attention to this principle—that (I give what I believe to be the literal and true rendering) "every prophecy of Scripture is not a matter to be interpreted of itself; for not by the will of man was prophecy of old time brought in, but it was spoken by holy men of God, carried along by the Holy Ghost."

In support of this translation I can here give only the following remarks.

i. The word ἐπίλυσις, "interpretation," does not occur in any other passage of the New Testament: but the verb ἐπιλύω, which means in classical Greek "to loose, untie, release," is used in Mark iv. 34, of Christ explaining or interpreting His parables to His disciples; and in Acts xix. 39, of a law question being disentangled or decided in a legal assembly. Hence "explanation" or "interpretation" seems to be the only rendering admissible.

ii. The meaning "private," given to ἴδιος in the Authorised Version, occurs elsewhere in the New Testament only in the phrase κατ' ἰδίαν, "in private," as used many times in the Synoptical

Gospels (e.g. Matt. xiv. 13, xiv. 23; Mark iv. 34; Luke ix. 10), also once in the Acts (xxiii. 19), and once in the Epistles (Gal. ii. 2). It is remarkable that in one of these passages (Mark iv. 34) it is in immediate connection with the word ἐπιλύω: but this can hardly be more than a chance coincidence. This signification, applying only to a single phrase, can hardly be accepted as giving us the true rendering here; and we must prefer the ordinary signification "own."

By saying that prophecy is not "a matter of its own interpretation," S. Peter would seem to draw a special distinction between it and all other writings. They, as it were, carry their own explanation, explicitly or implicitly, in themselves; it is simply a matter of study to find it there, and to understand them completely. But with prophecy it is otherwise. It contains mysteries which no human study or insight can penetrate: did we know the exact thought of the writer when he penned it, we should still be far from knowing its whole breadth and depth; which cannot be reached but by considering the whole purposes of God, and by special illumination from Him. This rendering gives a coherence to the whole passage; for he goes on to point out why this must be so, viz. because prophecy is the work not of man but of God. It came, he says, not by the will of man (as all mere human writings do); but it was spoken by holy men under the influence, the guiding and controlling power, of the Holy Spirit. A more distinct affirmation of a divine element pervading Scripture it would be hard to find. The twofold use of the word φέρω, "to bear or carry along," is worthy of note. Man's will was not the vehicle of the prophecy; but the Spirit was the vehicle of the men as they prophesied, carrying them along, so to speak, by an extraneous agency. At the same time the word itself teaches us that it is no mechanical necessity, no irresistible force, that is here spoken of: it is used of men leading an afflicted person, Mark vii. 32; viii. 22; of the power and motion of wind, Acts ii. 2; xxvii. 15; and generally of a gentle rather than a violent constraint.

We can now see how far the evidence, already summarized, for the existence of a divine element in the Bible is supported by these passages which specially deal with the subject. From the first passage, 1 Cor. ii. 12, 13, we learn S. Paul's belief as to his own preaching, and *à fortiori* as to his own writings—that, owing little or nothing to any mere human skill, they were delivered with demonstration of the Spirit and in the power of God: that their substance was revealed to him by God's Spirit, and their very words were not taught him by man's wisdom, but by the Holy Ghost. From the second passage, 2 Tim. iii. 14–17, we derive the name, and may almost frame a definition, of Inspiration. It is the breathing of a divine life into the framework of Scripture, as the living soul was breathed into the clay of Adam; a life which renders that Scripture profitable for reproof or for instruction, able to make the man of God both wise unto salvation and perfectly furnished for all good works. The third passage, 1 Peter i. 10–12, paints to us the conditions of consciousness under which the seers of the Old Testament delivered their prophecies; how urged by a power within them they spoke they knew not what, dim but splendid presages of the glory of some unknown future; and how, when they strove and prayed to see more clearly the place and the hour and the circumstances of those triumphs, there was borne to their souls a divine warning that these things were not for them to know, but were reserved to another and far-distant generation. The fourth and last passage, 2 Pet. i. 19 sqq. confirms and developes this idea; laying down distinctly that the writers of Scripture spake not of their own wills, but as they were moved by the Holy Ghost: and consequently that their writings are not, like others, to be explained by themselves alone, and on human principles of interpretation, but only from a due analysis of the whole message of God, and from what we know of his nature and of his dealings with man: but that so explained they form a more sure and certain ground of faith, than even the explicit testimony of eyewitnesses to the miracles of the new dispensation.

No further proof needs, I think, to be alleged that, if the New Testament is to be believed at all, the natural theory of Inspiration not merely fails in being a complete account of the genesis of the Bible, but that it wholly ignores its most essential and distinguishing features; that on the contrary all Scripture is to be looked upon as containing an actual Revelation, an authentic message from God, written down by the aid and direction of the Spirit; and that any imperfections which may arise from the human nature of the messengers must be matters of secondary and insignificant import, involving no sensible detraction from its generally supernatural character. Whether such imperfections do in fact exist we might now at once proceed to inquire, were it not that the present seems the most fitting occasion for stopping to consider a question, which has probably already occurred to the minds of most readers, and which it is impossible to leave altogether unanswered. It may be stated as follows:—*If the writers of the Old and New Testaments are inspired, why do they not, at the outset of their work, and at any other place where their authority might need support, assert definitely and distinctly their own Inspiration?* As they do not do so, must we not conclude that they were not conscious of any such supernatural influence?

This silence is no doubt a remarkable phenomenon, and one which, reasoning *à priori*, we should not probably have expected. But I believe consideration will show that it is strictly analogous with other facts of God's dealing with man, and in no way prejudices the reality of Inspiration: in short, that the question just asked admits of a full answer, and that the terms of that answer will actually supply further evidence in favour of a divine element in the Bible.

Before answering the objection it will be best to examine how far it actually holds, i.e. how far this silence as to Inspiration pervades the whole of the Canon. The result of this examination is as follows:

The whole of the Pentateuch and the other books of the Old Testament, as far as the second book of Kings, form one connected history of God's dealings with His chosen people from the beginning of the world. This history is strictly anonymous, the names of the writers even being nowhere given, much less any statement as to their character or inspiration. The First Book of Chronicles makes a break in the series, ascending once more to the beginning of time, but still gives no hint of its author. The book of Ezra begins in the same style, but in chap. vii, where Ezra's own credentials from the Persian king are quoted, he assumes the first person, and from thenceforward the book takes the form of a personal narrative. But though the author is thus made known to us, he says nothing whatever as to his inspiration. The book of

Nehemiah is of the same character, and with the same limitation. Job is distinctly a poem, of unknown authorship. The Psalms are throughout in the first person, but, as is natural in lyric poetry, without specifying their author, though this is in many cases known to us from other parts of the Bible, or from tradition. Proverbs is a collection of sayings of Solomon, with a few subjoined from other sources; Ecclesiastes is a didactic treatise, and the Song of Songs an elegy ascribed to the same author. Hitherto then we find nothing like a claim to Inspiration. When we come to the Prophets the case is different. Nothing can be more distinct than the way in which they continually assert themselves to be only the mouthpiece of the Divine Inspirer. The titles or commencements of the different books are enough in themselves to prove this. They are such as these: "The vision of Isaiah the son of Amoz, which he saw."—"The words of Jeremiah the son of Hilkiah .... to whom the word of the Lord came;"—"The word of the Lord came expressly unto Ezekiel the priest;"—"The word of the Lord that came unto Hosea;"—"the words of Amos which he saw;"—and so forth. And similar expressions, with others such as "thus saith the

Lord," "the Lord hath spoken it," are the constantly recurring burden of these books. At the same time there is some doubt as to the mode in which the prophecies, after being orally delivered, were committed to writing; and certainly but little express information on this head. We have, however, two special instances. One is in Isaiah viii. 1, where the prophet is instructed to "take a great roll and write in it concerning Maher-shalal-hash-baz." The other, which is much more circumstantial, is in Jeremiah xxxvi, the narrative of the roll of prophecies which the king Jehoiakim destroyed. We are there told that "this word came unto Jeremiah from the Lord, saying, Take thee a roll of a book, and write therein all the words that I have spoken unto thee against Israel, and against Judah, and against all the nations, from the day I spake unto thee, from the days of Josiah, even unto this day." It seems to follow from this that the prophecies of Jeremiah had not previously been written down, and that he was enabled by divine assistance to remember and to dictate the whole of the words, which he had from time to time spoken at his Lord's command. In verse 4 we are told how this injunction was carried out: "Baruch wrote from the mouth of Jeremiah all the words of the Lord, which he had spoken unto him, upon a roll of a book." This account is exactly reproduced in Baruch's own words to the princes in verse 18. This roll having been destroyed, Baruch, by God's command (verse 28), takes another roll and writes therein all the words of the former roll, as they were once more repeated to him by the mouth of the prophet; and, we are told, "there were added besides unto them many like words," so that we may fairly conclude this second roll to have been the original copy from which the present book of Jeremiah is derived. From this minute narrative we may gather three things: (1) that the messages of the Hebrew prophets were in the first place spoken and not written; (2) that they were afterwards written down, not always at the time, but certainly under the express sanction and direction of God; (3) that when so written down they were accepted, even by those who in deeds rejected the messenger and the message, as being in truth the words of Jehovah Himself. This view is implicitly supported by the writings of the other prophets, especially of Ezekiel, whose book is a regular series of short oral prophecies accurately and carefully recorded, with exact notes of time and circumstance. The commencement of chapter xxix may be taken as a typical instance. "In the tenth year, in the tenth month, in the twelfth day of the month, the word of the Lord came unto me, saying, Son of man, set thy face against Pharaoh, king of Egypt, and prophesy against him, and against all Egypt; speak, and say, Thus saith the Lord God." Hence, in general, we may say that the principle of the Old Testament is to give no hint as to Inspiration, and but few as to authorship, except in the case of prophecies of future events, when both are distinctly and emphatically asserted.

The usage of the New Testament is in entire accordance with this. S. Matthew and S. Mark's Gospels are wholly silent on the matter. S. Luke in his preface does not mention his own name, and grounds his motive for writing, not on any special inspiration of his own, but on the complete information he had received from men who were "eye-witnesses and ministers of the word." S. John, at the very end of his Gospel (xxi. 24), gives a hint as to his own identity; but he seems to rest his claims to be listened to on his own character for truthfulness, and his competency to record that which he had seen and heard. The Acts, as a historical document, reverts to the anonymous character of the Synoptic Gospels. In S. Paul's Epistles the authorship is never left in doubt (putting aside that to the Hebrews), since he always commences with his own name; and his claims to Apostleship are frequently insisted on, especially at the commencement; but direct claims to inspiration are undoubtedly rare, except in two Epistles, those to the Thessalonians. Here there are several passages in which S. Paul claims most distinctly to speak "by the word of the Lord" (see 1 Thes. ii. 13, iv. 1, iv. 2, iv. 15, 2 Thes. ii. 15, iii. 1, iii. 14). This peculiarity seems fully accounted for, when we remember that these were written first of all the Epistles, and comparatively early in S. Paul's ministry; so that it was natural for him to assert and emphasize claims, which were conceded to him beyond question or dispute by those to whom his later writings were addressed. In any case the fact remains that S. Paul does not as a rule make it any part of his work to dwell on his own inspiration; and the same holds true of the authors of the General Epistles. When we come to the last book of the Canon, the Apocalypse, the case is different. Here we have a work comparable with the prophetical books of the Old Testament, being the immediate record of a wholly supernatural communication; accordingly, S. John is careful to tell us that he was "in the Spirit on the Lord's day" when the great vision was vouchsafed to him: the short epistles to the seven churches are given as messages by "one like the Son of Man," and are also described as being what the Spirit says to the churches; and throughout the book we are never allowed to forget for one moment the supernatural nature of the occurrences, though, as in the Old Testament, the time and conditions of their being committed to writing are not declared to us. In all this the parallel between the usages of the two Testaments appears exact and complete.

Such then are the facts of the case, and they undoubtedly bear out the general statement that the writers of Scripture do not as a rule seek to impress on their readers the fact of their own inspiration. Are we to conclude from this that this inspiration did not exist? I think not. Apart from the precise, though infrequent statements which we do find on the subject, and which have been fully set forth in Part I of this treatise, several reasons may be given which justify us in attaching no weight to this objection. These I propose briefly to consider.

I. In the first place this silence is in strict analogy with a general rule which may be observed throughout the Bible; which is that all religious doctrines and underlying principles are not explicitly stated, but implicitly contained and implied. It is often said that no code of moral laws is to be found anywhere in the New Testament; still less is there any formulated statement of theology. The very greatest and most fundamental articles of the Christian faith—the Atonement, the Divinity of our Lord, the Trinity itself—are in no one place formally set forth. This is doubtless a strange phenomenon. The Bible differs therein from all other religious books, Jewish or heathen, and from anything which a human author would be likely to create; it becomes thereby not a dead text-book but a living guide. On this, however, I have no right to enlarge; but the fact I have stated is indisputable, and it clearly removes our surprise that the doctrine of Inspiration should be so obscurely stated, when we find that it thus falls under a general law, embracing all the leading principles of our faith.

II. The objection we are considering belongs to a class which proposes to lay down arbitrarily the nature and amount of evidence which is to be given in support of Revelation; a good example of which is the well-known aphorism, that if God had meant to give a revelation to men He would have written it for them in the sky. All such positions are untenable. That the principles of religion are not *absolutely certain*, as our own existence, or as the first truths of arithmetic are certain, is a fact so obvious that it is scarcely mentioned as a postulate in controversy. No writing on the face of heaven is necessary for such certainty; we might simply have had an inward conviction of its truth, as strong as that of our own existence. This has not been vouchsafed to us: and it is easy to see why. God's aim is not the convincing us of His own existence and attributes, but the teaching us to love and serve Him, to our own immeasurable gain. With such a certainty as I have described, free will would be useless, and service mechanical. But, once granted that the evidence for religion is short of certainty, and was designed so to be, and the ground of all these objections is cut away. For clearly we have no means of fixing *à priori* the exact degree of evidence to be afforded to us, more particularly as regards any one particular part of the scheme of religion; we cannot say, "this doctrine cannot be true, because, if it were, this or that evidence would have been given to make us believe it;" all that we can really inquire into is, whether the evidence which we do possess is as a whole sufficient to make it our duty to act on the assumption of its truth.

III. It may further be conjectured that even if the case were otherwise—if Inspiration was explicitly asserted throughout—this would by no means have the effect in producing conviction, which might at first sight be looked for. Suppose that every book in the Bible, of whatever character, opened with a solemn and express declaration that the writer was actuated by the Spirit of God. Would not this declaration itself be pointed to, as an indication that the writer was simply a daring impostor, trying to impress his hearers with a belief in his supernatural power? would not any such intimations on the subject, as we now find scattered through the books, be taken as intentional efforts to support the claim thus made at the outset? and would not any real or fancied error, however foreign to the subject and however small in itself, be held up as an irrefragable proof that the whole claim was nothing less than a lie? There would then be no middle course between complete acceptance and complete rejection of Biblical truth; and thousands of minds whose tendency is to doubt, but who, doubting, still cling to a long cherished faith, would then be driven at once into the ranks of avowed disbelief.

IV. Somewhat akin to observation No. II. is another, which it is necessary to dwell upon at greater length. All the books of the New Testament were written primarily to be read by certain classes of people existing at a particular epoch. It is only in a secondary sense that they are addressed to, and concern, the dwellers in other lands and other ages. This is a fact which Christians of all times have been prone to forget, and have always fallen into great and grievous error by forgetting it. But it is indisputable, and all sound criticism must be based upon it. Now it follows on this that the writers of the Bible never attempt to tell or to explain any fact, which those whom they were addressing were already familiar with. Such things are always taken for granted, and subsequent readers, who might not have the same knowledge, are left to discover the meaning as they can. To take one prominent example of this: 2 Thessalonians is full of allusions to teaching on certain very deep subjects, which S. Paul had delivered orally to the particular Church he was then addressing. Our ignorance of what that oral teaching had been makes it almost impossible for us to unravel all the obscurities of that letter. The very perplexing allusions to the gift of tongues, a phenomenon which, whatever its nature, was clearly a familiar one to the early converts, form another illustration of the fact. Now to apply this to the question of Inspiration. Those early Christians among whom the Apostles laboured, and to whom they wrote, were clearly the best judges as to whether those Apostles were really men inspired by the Spirit of God. That they did believe them so to be, their conversion is in itself no small evidence. And if this was so—if it was a matter of course, long ago established to the recipients of these Epistles, that their writers were men really "moved by the

THE NATURAL THEORY. 83

Holy Ghost,"—then it is against all analogy and all likelihood that this should be explicitly stated and dwelt upon in the course of those writings. This then is another and a weighty reason why we should not expect the assertion of Inspiration to occur prominently in the New Testament. But we may carry the argument further. If the inspiration, say of S. Paul, was thus an established truth to his converts—if any letter coming from him was sure of being unhesitatingly accepted as the word of God—then we should not expect him to proclaim his own inspiration where he felt it to exist; but we *should* expect him to be very careful and emphatic in noting any occasion (should such occur) when in the course of his writing he felt that that special guidance was withheld; and that he was merely speaking, like any other man, under the light of reason and experience. In brief *we should not look for assertions of inspiration, but we should look for avowals of non-inspiration.* And if any such are found, they will form evidence of the strongest possible character for belief in the general inspiration, not only of the particular book in which they occur, but of all others. Hence comes the question, *Are any such avowals of non-inspiration to be found in the writings of the New Testament?* I believe that there are.

The special case on which I rest this belief is chapter vii. of 1 Cor., which I propose to consider in some detail. That Epistle differs from all other Epistles in this, that it is in great measure (see 1 Cor. vii. 1) a reply: i.e. written by S. Paul, not of his own motion, but in answer to a letter received by him from the governing body of the Corinthian Church. This letter has not been preserved, and we can only conjecture its contents from those of the answer which was made to it. It is evident that it requested S. Paul's opinion upon a number of points, all of them rather of practical discipline than of spiritual life or abstract theology—on the general question of virginity and marriage, vii. 1; on the relations of a Christian wife to an unbelieving husband, or *vice versâ*, vii. 12; on the marriage of virgins, vii. 25; on the eating of things offered to idols, viii. 1; on the payment of ministers, ix. 1; on covering the head in church, xi. 1; on the use and relative value of spiritual gifts, xii. 1; on a collection for poor Christians, xvi. 1; and possibly on other points alluded to in the course of the Epistle. It will be seen that these are akin to a multitude of questions which have arisen in all ages of the Church—questions for which no direct answer is to be found in the Bible, and which each age has therefore been compelled to solve by the best means in its power. This leads to the conjecture that, with regard to such points of doubt in the Corinthian Church, it might seem fit to the wisdom of God to leave them to the same uncertainty—not to meet their interrogations with a direct reply, but let them seek their answer by the ordinary processes of reason and faith. Here then, if anywhere, we might expect to find in an inspired Epistle some uninspired passages. Starting with this *à priori* probability, let us turn to chap. vii, where, after much wise counsel on higher or deeper matters, S. Paul turns to consider the points of detail submitted to him. Having laid down certain rules as to the duties of married life, he breaks off to say (ver. 6), " But I speak this by permission, and not of commandment. For I would that all men were even as I myself. But every man hath his proper gift of God, one after this manner, and another after that. I say therefore to the unmarried and widows, It is good for them if they abide even as I. But, &c."

It may be thought that we have here at once a case in point. But careful study of the passage will show, I believe, that S. Paul is merely distinguishing between matters of command, and matters of permission. He is simply desirous to lay down the weighty principle (how much and sadly ignored!) that such questions as these upon the relative value of marriage and virginity are matters of time and season, to be decided by individual judgment, not by positive law; and that he is not thinking of any difference, as to Inspiration, between his teaching on this and on other points. If so, this is not a particular case of non-inspiration, such as we are seeking; at the same time it indirectly strengthens the general argument, because we have here a statement, not of a point of detail, on which guidance might be withheld, but of a great general truth, the need for which is sufficiently shown by the persistence with which it has been ignored.

Passing on from this, S. Paul gives (in vv. 8, 9) a general direction on the subject to the unmarried, evidently still within the region of assent or permission, and prefaced by the word λέγω, "I say." But in v. 10 he changes the verb abruptly to παραγγέλλω, "I enjoin or command," and then adds the remarkable words οὐκ ἐγώ, ἀλλ' ὁ Κύριος—the substance of the injunction being the great moral law that husband is not to separate from wife, nor wife from husband. This applies of course to all married persons whatsoever. He then seems to make a reference to special questions asked him by a particular class of his converts in reference to a branch of the same subject, and he does so in these words, Τοῖς δὲ λοιποῖς ἐγὼ λέγω, οὐχ ὁ Κύριος, "to the rest[1] say I, not the Lord;" and he then goes on (vv. 12–17) to consider the case of married couples of which one member only was a believer. It seems clear that a sharp distinction is meant to be drawn between παραγγέλλω and λέγω, between "I" and "the Lord;" and the question is, of what nature is this distinction.

There is an obvious answer to this question, which is supported by De Wette, Wordsworth, Alford, Lee, &c., in modern times, and by Chrysostom and Theodoret in ancient; and which makes the reference to be the well-known words

---

[1] One would expect these words to refer to the unmarried, as opposed to the married, to whom he had been previously speaking; but they may, I believe, be rendered "to those others who have asked my advice on this class of subjects."

of Christ, in which He asserted the indissoluble sanctity of the marriage tie. Οὐκ ἐγὼ, ἀλλ' ὁ Κύριος will therefore be, "not I, but the Lord Himself on earth." That this interpretation is incorrect I am not altogether prepared to assert; but, at the same time, there are more reasons against it than would appear at first sight; and it seems on the whole most probable that S. Paul is here contrasting an injunction delivered to him directly from his Lord in heaven with fallible words of his own. It will perhaps be well to discuss the point.

First, we have the striking fact that, as a rule almost without exception, S. Paul never appeals to the spoken discourses of our Lord to support his own statements or injunctions. In the Acts there is one solitary case (xx. 35), and there, curiously enough, the saying referred to is one not found in any of the Gospels. In the Epistles 1 Cor. xi. 23 is no real exception to the law, being an historical account of an institution, not an appeal to authority. There is, however, one passage, also in the present Epistle (ix. 14), which seems to be a reference, not indeed to actual words, but to an ordinance of Christ's on earth, expressed in the Gospels by the saying,

"The labourer is worthy of his hire." Still even here the matter is historical rather than didactic, showing how the ancient rules of the Law had been continued on to the times of the Gospel; and it scarcely therefore breaks the silence I have noted. Such a silence, it may be noted, supplies a strong argument for his belief in the sufficiency of his own supernatural gifts. At any rate, this is his uniform practice, and as no reason appears for his varying it here, we are bound, as it seems to me, to reject this view of the passage, unless no other can be found to take its place.

Secondly, supposing him to wish to refer to a saying of Christ's earthly ministry, would ὁ Κύριος (the Lord) be the word he would naturally employ? To determine this point, the passages in the Acts and Pauline Epistles in which that word occurs have been examined. The usage in both Acts and Epistles is much the same, and is as follows:— The expression ὁ Κύριος is used very frequently, much as we say "The Lord," as a synonymous term to God, without exactly defining any one of the Three Persons. It is also used frequently to mean our Lord, not however historically as He lived on earth, but as He now lives in heaven. Finally, it is occasionally, but rarely, used of our

Lord in His historical character. It is, however, remarkable that just half of the examples of this usage come from this same Epistle to the Corinthians. These are, 1 Cor. vi. 14 (ὁ Θεὸς καὶ τὸν Κύριον ἤγειρε); ix. 5 (οἱ ἀδελφοὶ τοῦ Κυρίου); ix. 14 (οὕτω καὶ ὁ Κύριος διέταξε); xi. 26 (τὸν θάνατον τοῦ Κυρίου). The other cases are Gal. i. 19, 1 Thess. i. 6, Heb. ii. 3, vii. 14. But in all these passages the context fully determines the sense, which is not the case here; and it would therefore seem most probable that if S. Paul, in the passage before us, had before his mind his Lord as an earthly teacher, he would have used some more distinctive title for Him. In any case we must note the remarkable order of the words—παραγγέλλω οὐκ ἐγὼ, ἀλλ' ὁ Κύριος, not οὐκ ἐγὼ, ἀλλ' ὁ Κύριος παραγγέλλει. Even if we adopt the last-named view of his meaning, that meaning has its lesson for us. It is not that he has no power to enjoin, or that his injunctions have any less weight than his Lord's; it is only that, where historically such an injunction had been given, he naturally refers to it, even as an earthly teacher might refer to some recognised authority, and as though he would say, "You need not have put to me this particular question, not that I am

THE NATURAL THEORY. 91

unable to decide it, but because it has been already decided for you by the words of our common Lord." In this case also v. 12 must be taken as putting his own sayings and those of Christ on an equal footing: "But to the rest speak I, not the Lord; if any brother hath a wife, &c." (Τοῖς δὲ λοιποῖς ἐγὼ λέγω οὐχ ὁ Κύριος· εἴ τις ἀδελφὸς γύναικα ἔχει.) But on the whole, the balance appears to be in favour of the view that he is contrasting a commandment of his Lord in heaven with his own opinion on earth; in other words, that he is disclaiming for the moment his own inspiration.

But a far stronger and clearer instance is that which follows in v. 25. S. Paul has just laid down as a general principle that Christian men and women were to abide in the same position in which they were called. He then passes on to the next question on his list—a question the exact terms of which it is not easy to restore, but which bore some reference to the giving in marriage or otherwise of marriageable maidens. It was a point to which the principle just laid down might seem to apply; and so apparently S. Paul does mean to apply it; but with how faltering and uncertain a tone, how unlike the firm utterance we have been listening to! These are his words: "Now concerning virgins, I have no commandment of the Lord; yet I give my judgment, as one that hath obtained mercy of the Lord to be faithful. I suppose therefore that this is good for the present distress, I say that is good for a man so to be." (Περὶ δὲ τῶν παρθένων, ἐπιταγὴν Κυρίου οὐκ ἔχω· γνώμην δὲ δίδωμι ὡς ἠλεημένος ὑπὸ Κυρίου πιστὸς εἶναι. Νομίζω οὖν τοῦτο καλὸν ὑπάρχειν διὰ τὴν ἐνεστῶσαν ἀνάγκην, ὅτι καλὸν ἀνθρώπῳ τὸ οὕτως εἶναι, &c.)

Now my contention is that here we have a distinct statement by S. Paul that he was not speaking under Inspiration—a statement made in as clear and unequivocal terms as he could possibly have used. That it should not have been generally so understood is in no wise wonderful, when we consider the strict views on Inspiration which, without any special inquiry, have been held in most ages of the Church. It is also rendered more likely by the superficial resemblance of the opening words to those of vv. 10, 12, which we have just been considering. Hence Bishop Wordsworth and others say that by ἐπιταγὴν Κυρίου οὐκ ἔχω, S. Paul means that Christ when on earth had given no commandment in this case, as He had in that of divorce. This plausible interpretation seems to be decisively negatived by the following considerations.

1. On this interpretation, ἐπιταγή must mean a commandment of Christ delivered when on earth. But, on referring to the places in which this word is used in the New Testament, it will be found that in no single instance does it bear this meaning. On the other hand, there are three passages (Rom. xvi. 26; 1 Tim. i. 1; Tit. i. 3) in which it is used of the ordinances of God from heaven, taking effect upon and in inspired men, exactly as it would be used here. So, too, the verb ἐπιτάσσω, which is used eight times in the Gospels, once in the Acts, and once in the Epistles, never bears the sense of a general didactic rule laid down, but of an imperative command to do some definite thing —to unclean spirits to come forth from the possessed, Luke iv. 36—to the winds and waves to sink into calm, Luke viii. 25—to the officers to smite S. Paul on the mouth, Acts xxiii. 2— and so forth. In fact, by this interpretation we are making ἐπιταγή usurp the place of another word which regularly and legitimately has this connotation, viz. ἐντολή; as may be seen in many

passages throughout the New Testament, including two in the present Epistle, vii. 19 and xiv. 37.

2. On this theory ἔχω must have here the sense of "have to refer to," or "have to produce." This is contrary to its use in the New Testament, which seems invariably to imply actual possession—"to hold" rather than "to have" simply; the nearest passage is perhaps 2 Cor. v. 12, ἵνα ἔχητε πρὸς τοὺς ἐν προσώπῳ καυχωμένους: but even here it is more definite in its character.

3. On this theory γνώμη must be taken to mean an inspired sentence or judgment pronounced by S. Paul himself, as opposed to a saying handed down from our Lord. Now the New Testament instances of this word are but few. We have Acts xx. 3, ἐγένετο γνώμη, "the opinion prevailed," or "the decision was come to;" 1 Cor. i. 10, ἐν τῇ αὐτῇ γνώμῃ, "of the same opinion;" 1 Cor. vii. 40, κατὰ τὴν ἐμὴν γνώμην, where the sense will be the same as here; 2 Cor. viii. 10, καὶ γνώμην ἐν τούτῳ δίδωμι, a most important passage, since the word is here clearly opposed to κατ' ἐπιταγὴν in v. 8, and the sense is, "I give my opinion merely on the matter in place of

THE NATURAL THEORY. 95

laying any injunction on you;" Philem. 14, χωρὶς δὲ τῆς σῆς γνώμης, "without your judgment in the matter;" lastly, three closely allied passages in Rev. xvii. (vv. 13, 17), where the ten horns are said to act with μία γνώμη, "one mind," and in thus acting to be in reality fulfilling the γνώμη or "mind" of God. We see that everywhere the clear connotation of the word is that of an opinion, a judgment formed upon the circumstances of a case and only to be taken for what it is worth, in distinct contrast therefore (in 2 Cor. viii. 10 an actual verbal contrast) with ἐπιταγή, ἐντολή, or any other word signifying "charge," "injunction," "command."

4. This is doubly confirmed by the use of the word νομίζω in verse 26. This word (except in one case, Acts xvi. 13, where it means "be accustomed") always signifies "to suppose," "to imagine," "to be of opinion," without any idea of authority or special knowledge; see, in the Gospels, Matt. v. 17, xx. 10, Luke ii. 44, iii. 23, and in the Acts vii. 25, viii. 20, xiv. 19, xvi. 27. The only two passages in the Epistles are the strongest of all. They are verse 36 of this very chapter, εἰ δέ τις ἀσχημονεῖν ἐπὶ τὴν παρθένον αὐτοῦ νομίζει, "If any man think that he behaveth himself uncomely

towards his virgin," where it is used of those very learners and converts to whom S. Paul is here writing; and 1 Tim. vi. 5, νομιζόντων πορισμὸν εἶναι τὴν εὐσέβειαν, "supposing that gain is godliness," where it is specially applied to men corrupt in their minds and turned away from the truth.

Looking at the words he employs, and especially at these two last, I fail to see how S. Paul could have more strongly, or more pointedly, inculcated the fact that he was not here delivering an infallible, dogmatic command, but merely expressing the judgment of his own fallible, erring reason. How utterly different is his tone from the emphatic and unfaltering way in which he everywhere else lays down principles or decides questions,—see, for example, 1 Cor. ii. 13; Gal. i. 11; 1 Thess. iv. 15; 2 Thess. iii. 14; Tit. i. 3—above all perhaps the striking passage in this present Epistle, xiv. 37, ἐπιγινωσκέτω ἃ γράφω ὑμῖν ὅτι Κυρίου εἰσὶν ἐντολαί, "Let him acknowledge that the things that I write unto you are the commandments of the Lord," where his own writings are asserted by him to be altogether equivalent to the ἐντολαὶ or commandments of his Lord. For this word ἐντολὴ, as already remarked, is the regular term for commands orally delivered whether by Christ or His apostles, and is used both by Himself (Matt. v. 19, xix. 17, John xiii. 34, &c.), and by others (Col. iv. 10, 1 Tim. vi. 14, 2 Pet. iii. 2, 1 John iii. 23, iv. 21). This passage, occurring as it does in the same Epistle as that we are considering, seems to conform strongly our view of the present passage, 1 Cor. vii. 25. We are therefore driven finally to conclude that S. Paul is here not thinking (as it was not his wont to think) of any need that words of his should gain as it were a prior sanction from spoken sentences of Christ on earth, but of a far different matter, namely, that they had at that moment no such sanction, as they were wont to have, from Christ in heaven. There lay no injunction on him from above, such as was ever present to make him speak boldly as he ought to speak, since he felt himself but the mouthpiece of his Lord; for once he was left to face out the difficulty, to meet it the best way he could by his own unassisted reasonings. And certainly in his mode of meeting it there is a great change from the firm and confident utterance to which we are accustomed in S. Paul. He lays down no principle, affirms no doctrine; he does not, as elsewhere, say boldly what is right, but suggests what is "good for the present necessity;" and this word "good" he repeats twice, with a sort of faltering altogether strange in him who wrote as "an Apostle, not of men, neither by man, but by Jesus Christ." This doubtful speech lasts, as it seems to me, through four verses; and then suddenly, without warning, comes surging back the full tide of Inspiration; and the Apostle, a true "apostle" or messenger, once more, breaks back from wandering in the thorny paths of doubtful opinion to the broad highway of grace, and throws out those high and stirring words which have been called the keynote of the whole Epistle. "But this I say, brethren ($\phi\eta\mu\grave{\iota}$, no longer $\nu o\mu\acute{\iota}\zeta\omega$), the time is short: it remaineth that both they that have wives be as though they had none, and they that weep as though they wept not, &c."

The last verse we have to consider on this subject is also the last verse of the chapter, verse 40: "But she is happier if she so abide, after my judgment: and I think that I also have the Spirit of God." (Μακαριωτέρα δέ ἐστιν ἐὰν οὕτω μείνῃ, κατὰ τὴν ἐμὴν γνώμην· δοκῶ δὲ κἀγὼ πνεῦμα Θεοῦ ἔχειν). Here we have repeated the word γνώμη, which we have considered just above; and we have also the marked expression πνεῦμα Θεοῦ ἔχειν. What then is the sense of this passage? S. Paul, in the nine verses following the burst of eloquence we have just quoted, has been speaking gravely and soberly of the advantages which a single life offers for active and unimpeded service to God, specially guarding himself throughout against being supposed to lay down principles or commands of universal application. In verse 39 he apparently passes from the question of virginity to another, which had been asked him on a kindred subject—that of second marriage—and disposes of it briefly and decisively. A woman may not marry again while her husband lives; when he is dead she is free to do so, "only in the Lord." So far there is no doubt or hesitation. He then goes on to say that she is happier (or rather "more blessed") without such second marriage—but adds instantly that this is according to his own opinion merely, not therefore a statement by authority. So far it would seem as if we had clear evidence of another case of non-inspiration, similar to that of verse 25; but the concluding words make this more doubtful. In interpreting these words Bishop Wordsworth says that δοκῶ means "I wot," said with a feeling of conscious dignity, and quotes a remark of Augustine (Tract. 37 in Joannem), "increpabat non dubitabat." On this view πνεῦμα Θεοῦ ἔχειν must mean "to be inspired," and S. Paul is defending against possible gainsayers the fact of his own Inspiration. That he is thinking here of those factious opponents whom he is clearly combating in chapter ix, and still more directly throughout the Second Epistle, I do not doubt; but that it is his immediate inspiration which he is maintaining appears to me to be conclusively negatived by the following considerations.

(1) The use of the expression κἀγώ, standing where it does, compels us, it would seem, to give the literal translation of the passage as follows: "And I think (or wot, or suppose) that *I as well as others* have the Spirit of God." Did καὶ stand alone we might take the meaning to be that besides his own opinion S. Paul believed he had divine Inspiration to back him; this, however, would be wholly opposed to that clear and perfect conviction of divine guidance which he everywhere else expresses. Or if ἐγὼ stood alone we might adopt Bishop Wordsworth's view and translate, " I wot that I (I at any rate, if no one else) am inspired by God." But the combination of the two seems to render any translation,

other than that just given, impossible. But if so, and if S. Paul be contrasting himself with his opponents at Corinth, "to have the Spirit of God" cannot mean "to be inspired;" for we cannot suppose that he meant to credit them with Inspiration; we do not even know that they made such an assertion themselves. It must refer to something as to which S. Paul might claim that he should at least be ranked on an equal footing with his opponents.

(2) What this is seems to be clearly brought out by an examination of the phrase Πνεῦμα ἔχειν. It is not once used (or any kindred phrase) of Inspiration. Far from this, it is used in the Gospels (Mark ix. 17, Luke iv. 33) of those who were possessed by evil spirits. It is true that in John xx. 22 our Lord says to His apostles, Λάβετε Πνεῦμα ἅγιον, "Receive ye the Holy Ghost:" but exactly the same phrase is used (Acts viii. 15, 17) of the whole of the infant Church of Samaria, to each member of which we cannot suppose plenary Inspiration to have been given. In Heb. vi. 4 lapsed Christians are spoken of as having been μέτοχοι Πνεύματος Θεοῦ, "partakers of the Holy Ghost." Lastly, to settle the matter, S. Paul in this very Epistle

uses exactly the same expression of the whole Church of Corinth, of those whose errors and shortcomings he so unsparingly denounced, those who had written to him for advice, and to whom he is now imparting his own inspired counsels: see 1 Cor. vi. 19, "the Holy Ghost which is in you, which ye have of God," (τοῦ ἐν ὑμῖν ἁγίου Πνεύματος, οὗ ἔχετε ἀπὸ Θεοῦ). It is plain then that the phrase refers to those ordinary "gifts of the Holy Ghost" which were wont to be bestowed on all converts alike, and that it is to a full share in these alone that S. Paul is here asserting his claim.

(3) This is further confirmed by considering the New Testament use of the word δοκεῖν, followed by an infinitive referring to the person who is the subject of this sentence. This use is fourfold:—

(i) In the ordinary classical sense of "to seem," Acts xvii. 18, 2 Cor. x. 9, Heb. iv. 1, James i. 26, probably Luke viii. 18 (καὶ ὃ δοκεῖ ἔχειν).

(ii) In the meaning of "think to do," or "think of doing something," as Matt. iii. 9 ("think not to say within yourselves"), 1 Cor. xi. 16, Phil. iii. 4.

(iii) In the sense of "to think that something is true," "to suppose, or deem," as Luke xxiv. 37

("supposed that they had seen a spirit"), John xvi.
2, Acts xii. 9, xxvi. 9, xxvii. 13, 1 Cor. viii. 2, x.
12, Gal. vi. 3.

(iv) In the sense of "to be looked on as," to "bear the repute of," or "be esteemed as" being something, Mark x. 42 (οἱ δοκοῦντες ἄρχειν), Luke xxii. 24, 1 Cor. iii. 18, xiv. 37, Gal. ii. 2 (τοῖς δοκοῦσι), ii. 6, ii. 9.

It will be noticed that in none of these cases does the word bear the strong affirmative sense ("I wot," "I am sure") which Bishop Wordsworth would give it in the present passage. The first sense (i) is clearly inapplicable; and so also is (ii), which could not precede such a verb as ἔχειν. We are thus confined to (iii) or (iv), and whichever we choose the Apostle's meaning will be nearly the same, viz. that he claims for himself a position which he feels sure must be conceded to him, the position of having received, no less than other Christians, the gift of the Divine Spirit, so that his γνώμη, or "opinion," is at least entitled to as much respect as theirs, though they both fall short of the direct and sure teaching of God. Probably (iii) is the correct meaning, especially since it agrees with the use of the word only two verses lower down (εἰ δέ τις δοκεῖ εἰδέναι τι); and the verse would then stand thus in modern phraseology, "But she is more blessed if she remain as she is, according to my individual judgment; and I presume that I too (as well as others) have received the Spirit of God."

These two passages (verses 25 and 40) are all which I have to bring forward (if we consider v. 12 to be doubtful,) as instances of non-inspiration found in an inspired document. There is another passage which at first sight presents the same appearance, i.e. that remarkable outburst in the Second Epistle to the Corinthians (ch. xi.), where S. Paul, speaking, as he says, not "after the Lord," (κατὰ Κύριον), but "as it were foolishly," describes his own great doings and sufferings for the cause of Christ. But the phrase κατὰ Κύριον can hardly be brought to apply to the subject of Inspiration. It is not elsewhere found in the Pauline Epistles; but its co-relative κατ' ἄνθρωπον is found five times, and means "after a human standard," or "in human relations," see Rom. iii. 5, 1 Cor. iii. 3, xv. 32, Gal. i. 11, iii. 15. There is another phrase, ἐν Κυρίῳ, which is very frequently used to express "in the name of the Lord," or "under the guidance of the Lord," and which we should have expected to find here if such had been the Apostle's thought at the moment. The general sense would therefore seem to be, "This language is not such as the Lord would use, not after the divine standard; but I am constrained for the moment to speak after a human fashion, even like those foolish persons (ἄφρονες) who are always commending themselves in a confidence of boasting."

In conclusion of this somewhat tedious inquiry, I seem to myself to have established that in at least two passages of a particular Epistle, wherein he was answering a set of questions on points of detail in Church polity, S. Paul finds himself without that express direction of the Spirit on which he was wont to lean ; and that so finding himself he at once takes pains to warn his readers of the fact by the use of language which, though it may require a certain amount of elucidation now, would have been perfectly clear and unequivocal in the ears of those to whom it was addressed. This proves both that S. Paul was himself a firm believer in his own general and plenary Inspiration, and that no argument against the reality of such Inspiration can be drawn from the silence of Scripture writers.

PART II.

SECOND LIMITING THEORY OF INSPIRATION.—THE LITERAL.

THE first part of the work has gone to prove that the New Testament witnesses of itself frequently, clearly, and beyond possibility of doubt, that it has in it a divine element, a weighty and authentic message delivered from God to men. We have now to inquire—Does the divine element altogether exclude the human? does the Bible contain this message of Revelation and nothing else? in other words, is it word for word dictated by the Spirit of God?

As remarked in the introduction, there are probably few persons of learning at the present day who would accept this opinion when thus explicitly stated; but there are very many who nevertheless hold it implicitly, inasmuch as they everywhere refuse to admit that any particular statement can be other than absolutely true, and a faithful reflection of the mind of God. It is these persons whom I would ask to join sincerely in the succeeding inquiry, begging them to remember from the outset that I am only doing what themselves demand that all men should do, viz. searching the Scripture of God in order to discover what it bids me believe of itself.

Now the first point to be ascertained must be:—

i. Do we find passages explicitly asserting that the Bible is dictated by the Spirit?

This must unquestionably be answered in the negative. There are no explicit assertions in the Bible as to the limits of the divine and human elements: like so many other points which *à priori* we should expect to be settled by authority, it is left to be cleared up by study and investigation. This has in fact been sufficiently shown above, in the inquiry as to the reasons why the Scripture writers do not assert explicitly their own Inspiration. It must be allowed however that the absence of such statements is a fact greatly to the disadvantage of the literal theory.

But we may proceed to inquire:—

ii. Are there a sufficient number of passages which, though not distinctly asserting the truth of the doctrine, do yet implicitly contain it, in such a way that we are bound to accept it as being the actual teaching of the Bible?

The passages which bear on this inquiry have been for the most part cited at the beginning of Part I. It will be well however to reconsider them now with special reference to our present point. The strongest are perhaps those in which Christ or His apostles cite the Old Testament with such expressions as "It is written;" of which the narrative of the Temptation affords a typical instance. But in almost all such instances the words quoted are from an actual Revelation or spoken message of God to men, of which the Old Testament forms merely the record. Of the existence and authenticity of such Revelations there is supposed to be no question among those who read this work: but it is clear that all which such citations guarantee is the fact of the Revelation, and the truthfulness of its record; they cannot prove the literal Inspiration of the whole book from which they are derived.

There are a few passages of a somewhat exceptional character which it will be well to discuss separately.

Mat. xiii. 35, "That it might be fulfilled which

was spoken by the prophet, saying, I will open my mouth in parables, &c."

This citation from the Psalms can scarcely mean more than to show that the same mode of imparting truth (by figures and parables), was familiar to the old dispensation and to the new: that in this as in other things the prophets forshadowed the action of the Messiah. In any case there can be no doubt that the Psalms are always represented as having been composed under direct spiritual and prophetic influence; and all that the citation implies is that under such influence the writer found himself called upon to use the same method of instruction as Christ used centuries afterwards.

Mat. x. 19, "But when they shall deliver you up, take no thought how or what ye shall speak: for it shall be given you in that same hour what ye shall speak: for it is not ye that speak, but the Spirit of your Father which speaketh in you."

This passage, important and striking as it is, is clearly a supreme promise, given for moments of supreme need. Nor even here does it necessarily imply that actual *words* were to be dictated, as is shown more clearly by the parallel passage, Luke xii. 12, where the expression is, "The Holy Ghost shall *teach* you in the same hour what ye ought to say." The difference between teaching and dictation may in fact be well used to illustrate the difference between the ideas of *plenary* and of *literal* Inspiration; in the one case knowledge is transfused from one mind into another as an active principle; in the other, the recipient is nothing more than a living phonograph, the mechanical recorder of individual facts.

John xiv. 26, "The Comforter . . . shall teach you all things, and bring all things to your remembrance, whatsoever I have said unto you."

I have already spoken of the supreme value of this saying, as assuring us that we have in the Gospels a faithful and trustworthy record of Christ's discourses while on earth; but the idea conveyed is by no means that of a literal word-for-word dictation, but of a supernatural quickening of the apostles' human memories, so as to enable them to recall vividly and distinctly the scenes of their Master's teaching, and hear again the echo of those gracious words which were ever proceeding out of His lips. But in the case of the clearest and most accurate recollection there is always the possibility of slight lapses as to immaterial details, such as might well escape the attention fixed on the wonder of the spoken word; and should such lapses be proved to exist in the Gospel records, this will therefore be no contradiction of the great promise given above.

Acts iv. 25, "Who by the mouth of Thy servant David hast said, Why do the heathen rage, &c."

This is a type of a class of passages (already given in Part I), where God or the Spirit is said to speak by or through a prophet. It is clear that in these we have the Divine element most specially and distinctly asserted, yet not so as to extinguish altogether the human. Though there is a Divine message, there is still a human messenger; God speaks, but it is by the mouth of a man. And as a king would be said to speak through his envoy, so long as that envoy delivered the true substance of his instructions, though in words and phrases of his own; so here, though the message itself must be accepted as coming from heaven, it may yet bear in the form it presents certain minor imperfections, caught from the imperfect channel through which it has been conveyed.

It may perhaps be noted here that in many passages which seem to belong to this category, viz. where the word λέγει (says) or even εἴρηκε (has spoken) is used without an expressed subject, and followed by a quotation from Scripture, the real subject is probably not Θεὸς, but ἡ γραφὴ used in that personified sense which I have distinguished as No. 2, in the dissertation on the use of the word γραφὴ, Part I, p. 51.

Rom. iii. 2, "To them were committed the oracles of God." The same remarks apply to this as to the last passage. The use of the word λόγιον, here and in three other passages (Acts vii. 38; Heb. v. 12; 1 Pet. iv. 11), most certainly implies the fact of an actual Revelation, given by God to His people in the Old Testament; but it does not prove (perhaps no single word could) that the book enshrining that Revelation is, in all places and throughout, a perfect product of infallible wisdom.

1 Cor. ii. 13, "Which things we speak, not in the words which man's wisdom teacheth, but which the Holy Ghost teacheth; comparing spiritual things with spiritual."

Here we have certainly the strong expression that the Spirit Himself teacheth not the things only, but the words which the apostles were to utter. But, besides recalling the distinction already drawn between teaching and dictation, we may observe that the whole context proves that S. Paul is here speaking of spiritual things, things "freely given to us of God;" hence, while we may gladly accept the assurance that on such matters the words of Scripture are the words of God Himself, we have no warrant here for extending the same to matters concerning the natural man, and needing no spiritual discernment.

1 Tim. iv. 1, "Now the Spirit speaketh expressly that in the latter times some shall depart from the faith, &c." Here again is a strong expression, the "speaking" of the Spirit (or rather "saying," for the Greek word is λέγει, though strengthened by the adverb ῥητῶς); but we must observe that the reference is to the prophecy by inspired Christians of future events; and such prophecy, if it exist at all, must clearly have its source directly in God's Spirit, and may therefore be directly attributed to Him.

2 Tim. iii. 15–17, "Of a child thou hast known the holy Scriptures, which are able to make thee wise unto salvation, &c."

We have already considered at length this great passage, and shown its bearing on the *reality* of Inspiration. At present we need only observe that it does not in any way define its *extent;* and also that all the objects enumerated for which Scripture is serviceable are spiritual objects, such as would be in no way affected by the truth or falsehood of literal Inspiration.

We come next to the Epistle to the Hebrews, which is remarkable for its numerous citations from the Old Testament, and for the bearing of many of these passages upon Inspiration. In the first three chapters (i. 5-7; ii. 11; iii. 7), we have three passages in which all three Persons of the Trinity are severally represented as saying words which are found in the Old Testament Scriptures; and these are confirmed by others, such as v. 5; ix. 8; x. 15, 30. But it will be found that all these citations are not merely extracts from books of the Old Testament: they bear on their face, as they occur, marks of being actual and immediate revelations of God. Thus, of the citations in i. 5-7, one is from an actual message sent by God through the prophet Nathan to David, 2 Sam. vii. 14; and the others are from Psalms (ii. 7; xlv. 6; xcvii. 7; civ. 4), which are universally recognised as the outpourings of a direct prophetic spirit in a lyric form. The same applies to the words ascribed to the Son in Heb.

THE LITERAL THEORY. 115

ii. 12, and cited from Ps. xxii. 22; and to the saying of the Holy Ghost given in Heb. iii. 7, and taken from Ps. xcv. 7. In Heb. iv. 4 we have a quotation from Genesis (ii. 2), "for he spake in a certain place of the seventh day on this wise; And God did rest the seventh day from all His works." But here again this expression, whatever its exact import, can only have been communicated to Moses by a supernatural intimation, and may therefore properly be ascribed to the Divine voice. The same law will be found to apply to the other passages given, e.g. Heb. x. 30, where the citation is from Deut. xxxii. 35, part of the inspired hymn which was to conclude the long roll of teachings and warnings addressed by Moses to the people of God. Generally, then, we may affirm that these passages in Hebrews tell us nothing as to the Scriptures of the Old Testament being throughout a literal message from God; but do tell us that they contain faithful records of certain special messages which were actually sent by Him to His people of old.

Lastly, we have two passages of S. Peter (1 Pet. i. 10; 2 Pet. i. 19), which have already been considered at length. These however are seen at once to be concerned only with *prophecy*, which, as before stated, must come immediately from God; and hence, while so far of the greatest value, give us no further help as to the literal Inspiration of Scripture in general.

Here ends our review of the passages in the New Testament most favourable to the literal theory; and it does not seem possible to draw from it any other conclusion than this: that while Prophecy and Revelation are very distinctly said to come straight from God, there is not a single statement, direct or indirect, that the Bible as a whole, or the parts of it which do not form a revelation of things beyond the knowledge of man, are absolutely dictated by Him. We cannot go further without asking the question, whether, if this be so, we are justified in assuming for a moment that it is so dictated? whether we are not rather deserting the Scriptures, our own chosen guide, setting up our own notions of what should be, instead of seeking what is, and claiming of God more than He has seen fit to give us? whether, in a word, it is not our duty to accept what the Bible tells us, and ask for no more?

We must not however omit to notice one other method by which the truth of the literal theory might conceivably be established; viz. by *à priori* arguments, proving its truth independently of Scripture testimony altogether. It may be admitted that the New Testament does not directly negative the literal theory, any more than it directly asserts it; and therefore a proof of this kind, if it could be adduced, might possibly be valid even to those who acknowledge the paramount authority of Scripture. But when we come to seek for such arguments, all that we can find appear to turn the other way. Thus we may say (i) that the literal theory is *unnecessary*. For the purpose of the Bible, as all admit, is, by the revelation of the whole "mystery of Godliness," to teach men to save their own souls and those of others. But it is clear that for this purpose no accurate instruction in science or history, no infallible dicta upon any matters of mere natural knowledge, are necessary; and therefore, since all analogy shows us that God does not, in any department of His work, waste power by doing more than is needful, we are rather bound to conclude that this literal dictation will *not* be found to be the true state of the case, than that it will. Again (ii) the Bible, as we now possess it, is certainly not an exact and literal message from God. Its essence, like that of all literature, is of course its *thoughts*, the conceptions it raises in the minds of those who receive it: but these conceptions are first clothed in language, and then written down in words and sentences, and then translated (as far as the greater part of mankind are concerned) into other languages, and then printed, and then handed down through years and centuries in countless successive copies; and in every one of these processes there must occur a certain amount of change, which must necessarily render the work, as we have it now, an imperfect one. But if so, for what end should it have been made perfect at first? Ought we not rather to expect that, as the weakness and imperfection of all earthly things could not fail to touch the work in its progress, so they would not be altogether absent from its origin?

Hitherto we have been considering the evidence that may be alleged in favour of the literal theory: we have now to inquire into the counter-evidence that may be brought forward against it. Although, as already mentioned, no explicit denial of the theory is to be found in the New Testament, this by no means implies that such counter-evidence does not exist. On the contrary, it is to be found in sufficient strength to constitute something approaching to an actual disproof of the doctrine. It is true that it is, by the nature of the case, somewhat subtle and minute in its character; but this does not impair, but may be said rather to enhance, its force. It resembles in fact those "undesigned coincidences" of which such powerful use has been made by Paley, Blunt, and others, in order to establish the historical truth both of the Old and New Testaments.

This evidence will be found to divide itself into two heads. (I) Traces of human *thought*, human motives, uncertainty, doubt, in the minds of the writers. (II) Traces of human *error*, mistakes as to time or place, inaccuracies in minor details, ignorance of scientific and historical truth, &c.

(I) *Traces of human thought.*

The first passage we shall adduce is Luke i. 1, where the historian gives the reason which induced him to undertake his task, viz. that he felt himself to have, from his opportunities, special qualifications for doing what many others were attempting to do, i.e. to give a full and accurate account of those things which were most surely believed by all. This might be the exordium to any work of contemporary history; the motive is doubtless praiseworthy, and there is no reason why God might not vouchsafe to bless with the gift of Inspiration a work commenced in such a spirit. But it seems almost impossible to believe that we have here the actual words of Divinity; that the Holy Spirit is making something like an apology for giving to mankind an authoritative record of the work of their salvation: or that a man who really felt himself to be nothing but the organ of an irresistible influence should go out of his way to dwell on motives far less direct and far less powerful.

Luke ii. 37, "A widow of *about* eighty-four years (ὡς ἐτῶν ὀγδοήκοντα τεσσάρων)[1]." To the Spirit of God all things, the smallest as well as the greatest, must be equally open and certain; there can be no room for even the faintest expression of doubt. We cannot conceive Him therefore as dictating such an expression. This, however small a matter in itself, is thus of value, as showing (1) that the *human* mind of the author is here at work, conscientiously marking that a statement is being

---

[1] Dr. Westcott has suggested, in a letter to the writer, that the usage is the same as when we say "about 3 miles from Paddington to King's Cross;" but age differs from distance, inasmuch as it is supposed to remain constant from one year to another. Certainly we should ourselves say, "about 84," only if we were not certain whether the age might not be 83 or 85.

made of which he is not positively certain ; (2) that the narrative itself is a *true* one, since nobody would trouble themselves as to accuracy on such a point when merely delivering a legendary or fictitious tale.

John ii. 6, "Holding two or three firkins apiece, (ἀνὰ μετρητὰς δύο ἢ τρεῖς.)" This is a case similar to the last, and seems clearly to indicate that we have here the words of an *eye-witness*; of a man recalling to his memory, somewhat vaguely after the lapse of years, the apparent size of the stone jars whose contents he had seen undergo that marvellous change, and forming in his mind a rough estimate of how much they would hold, to guide the imagination of his readers [1].

John vi. 19, "When they had rowed about five and twenty or thirty furlongs (ὡς σταδίους εἰκοσιπέντε ἢ τριάκοντα)." The observations made on the two last passages apply with equal exactness here; and we may note further that the fisherman, accustomed to measure with the eye his boat's distance from the shore of his own lake, but not accustomed to gauge the contents of water jars,

---

[1] Here also the word "about" cannot indicate an approximation merely: we do not say "about two or three," but "about two" or "about three."

gives his estimate within much more narrow limits on this than on the former occasion (two or three firkins), though the number is both in itself larger, and much more difficult of admeasurement to ordinary eyes; as all who have tried to judge distances over water are well aware. No doubt however he would be here assisted by his recollection of the time they had taken on that memorable night in rowing to the spot where their Lord met them; although the storm under which they laboured must have made that time exceptional.

1 Cor. i. 16, "Besides, I know not whether I baptized any other." Taking these verses (14–16) together, we have a singularly clear picture of a perfectly candid human mind struggling with the uncertainty of its own memory. In the midst of his eager expostulation against the "dividing of Christ," S. Paul thanks God that he had himself baptized none at Corinth but Crispus and Gaius; and is already proceeding with the thread of his argument (v. 15) when the "household of Stephanas" flashes across his memory. He pauses therefore to correct himself so far; and then, fearing lest some other case might still escape his recollection, adds the saving clause

we have quoted, and then throws himself once more into the argument at the point where he left it, "for Christ sent me not to baptize, &c."

2 Cor. xii. 2, 3, "Whether in the body I cannot tell, or out of the body I cannot tell, &c." In this very obscure passage we have S. Paul declaring himself ignorant of the nature or machinery of certain supernatural visions, vouchsafed either to some other, or (as most commentators hold) to himself. This is no place to discuss the point; but whatever view be taken of it, it seems very hard to make such an expression as this fit in with any theory approaching to that of Literal Inspiration.

The above list of passages may very probably be added to by more diligent search; the very minuteness of the criticism involved making its objects liable to be overlooked. It is submitted however that they are sufficient, taken together, to establish the fact that such "thinking for themselves" is found, rarely no doubt as in the nature of the case it would be, with the writers of the New Testament; and it must be remembered that even a single case of the kind, if fully established, would be sufficient to disprove the absolute truth of the literal theory.

(II) *Traces of human error, mistakes, inaccuracies, ignorance, &c.*

On this branch of the subject, which is of course of the highest importance, and in fact underlies the whole question of Inspiration, we shall not attempt to enlarge. The reason is that the work has been already done to our hand, in the valuable work of the late George Warington, "The Inspiration of Scripture; its limits and effects." Examples of error (trivial no doubt, but real) in the writings both of the Old Testament and New Testament are to be found everywhere in his book, but especially in his chapter on "Internal Testimony, indirect." To reproduce the whole of this would be useless. It may be well however to give one or two examples: and indeed one or two examples should suffice, because even a single case, if proved and admitted, is sufficient to overthrow the literal theory. The Holy Spirit cannot err, either in what He says, or what He dictates; therefore the existence of any error, forming an authentic part of a sacred writing, proves that there is in that writing some other element besides the dictation of the Spirit.

In choosing examples of discrepancies I am of course careful to select such as cannot be explained by their being really accounts of different though similar events. I am willing to attach full weight to this argument in many cases, notably as to variations in spoken words of our Lord. It is inconceivable that He should not, in His three years of teaching, have taken occasion to repeat many times the same great lessons in similar though not the same words; the mere fact of such repetition would tend to ensure those lessons being reproduced in the teaching and writings of His apostles, while at the same time each of them would very probably record a different occasion of their being delivered. In the following cases however no such explanation is feasible.

The first is shown by a comparison of Matt. x. 7 with Mark vi. 8. In each chapter we have a narrative of the same event, the calling together of the twelve disciples, and the giving them for the first time a commission to go forth and preach the kingdom apart from their Master. That this is the same occasion is proved beyond a doubt by the language of Matt. x. 5 and Mark vi. 7, both of which imply that this was the *first* time that such a mission took place; and also by the fact that in both cases it follows at the end of a journey through the "cities and villages," which is itself commenced almost immediately after the healing of the centurion's daughter. The charges addressed to the departing apostles are also, so far as they are common to both Gospels, almost identical; but there is this difference: that in Matt. x. 7, among the things that they were forbidden to take, we have "neither two coats, neither shoes, *nor yet staves*:" while in Mark vi. 8 the general command is given as being "to take nothing for their journey *save a staff only*." The word is the same in both cases (ῥαβδός); and it cannot be denied that what is forbidden in the one case is expressly excepted in the other. It is of course easy to say that the matter is a trivial one; easy also to show (as is done, e.g. by Wordsworth) that the sense is really the same in both cases. But the point remains the same, which is that our Lord must have used one expression or the other, and that therefore one account or the other must be to this extent inaccurate.

Our next example is the account of the healing of the centurion's servant, recorded in Matt. viii. 5–13, and in Luke vii. 1–10. That the incidents in both cases are the same is proved (1) by their being both stated to have happened on the occasion of Christ entering into Capernaum immediately after the Sermon on the Mount; (2) by the close and remarkable parallelism in the details, especially the objection of the centurion to Jesus coming into his house, and Jesus' astonishment and comment thereon. Nevertheless in these details there is this remarkable difference. According to S. Matthew the centurion came *himself*. We are told so distinctly in ver. 5 ("a centurion came unto Him, beseeching Him," &c.); it is assumed throughout the conversation, and is fixed beyond a doubt by the conclusion, "and Jesus said unto the centurion, Go thy way" (ὕπαγε, in the singular). In S. Luke we find, on the contrary, that the centurion "sent unto Him the elders of the Jews;" that *they* "besought Him instantly, saying that he was worthy for whom He should do this;" that Jesus went with *them;* and that when He was not far from the place the centurion sent to meet Him other friends, saying unto Him, "Lord, trouble not thyself; for I am not worthy that thou shouldest come under my roof; *wherefore neither thought I myself worthy to come unto thee.*" It is hard to see how a distinct contradiction as to fact (though doubtless on a minor point, not affecting the main truth or value of the story) could be more clearly established than by the foregoing.

In these two cases it is of course *possible* to maintain that two different events are alluded to. We will therefore take one more, where no one can maintain such a position; for it refers to the order of events in the last supper of Christ and His disciples, on the night of the betrayal. The three synoptic evangelists all agree in attributing to Christ on that occasion the mysterious words, "I will in no wise drink of the fruit of the vine until that day when I drink it new in the kingdom of God." But Matt. (xxvi. 29) and Mark (xiv. 25) agree in placing the words immediately after the benediction of the cup at the institution of the Sacrament; while Luke (xxii. 18) connects it with a previous division of a cup, and with words of similar purport as to the eating of the passover, which no other evangelist has recorded. It cannot be but that in one or the other account the saying is given out of its proper place.

That there *are* traces of human error in the New Testament is, I believe, sufficiently proved even by these three examples; as to their number, importance, and character, I shall have something more to say in Part III, and may meanwhile refer the reader to the work of Warington, from which the above cases are extracted.

PART III.

ATTEMPT TO FIX THE LIMITS OF INSPIRATION.

WE have now examined the two extreme theories with regard to Inspiration; (1) the natural theory, which recognises nothing beyond the ordinary care and direction which we believe God to exercise over all works done in His name; (2) the literal theory, which regards the Bible as a mere transcript of the direct words of the Holy Spirit. Both of these theories we have found to be disproved when judged of by the witness of the Bible itself, especially of the New Testament. We have thus found, in mathematical language, a superior and inferior limit for the Inspiration of the Scriptures; and it remains to discover whereabouts between these two limits the true place of Inspiration is to be found.

It is evident that this is by far the most difficult part of the inquiry. For in the two former cases we had before us definite and simple theories, and all that was needed was to bring them to the test of fact: but here we have to find a true theory for ourselves, either by collating and analysing all the facts, until from them we are able to deduce some one theory which approves itself as the true one; or by taking some hypothesis as our guide, testing it by facts as in the two former cases, and, if it fails, displacing it by another, to be submitted to the same process. Of these two methods the first is the more scientifically correct, but incomparably the more difficult of application. Accordingly, all attempts of the kind, whether in this or in other cognate subjects, have proceeded on the second method. Thus Warington suggests the principle that Inspiration extends only to things spiritual, not to things temporal; and much can be alleged to support this view. The weak point of such a principle is that, even if proved to be correct, it still leaves us in the difficulty of having to decide what is spiritual and what is temporal, a difficulty not easily overcome. It is clear we must not decide it by assuming those parts of the Bible which are inspired to be spiritual, and *vice versâ*; for this would be to argue in a circle. And how to draw the line by any other rule does not appear. It seems also very doubtful whether such an hypothesis, disputable as it is in itself, could ever be proved by an inquiry of this kind to the satisfaction of any who did not on *à priori* grounds believe it at starting. It seems far better, therefore, to assume at first nothing, but to begin with some principle which will by all reasonable men be admitted to be true; to apply this to the facts and see whether they cohere with it; and then by the light thus obtained advance to further positions, if such advance should seem to be warranted.

Now there is a principle of this kind which may well form the starting point of this inquiry, and which may be termed perhaps the *Principle of Divine Economy*. It may be thus stated: It is to be expected that God will give all such aid as is *necessary* for the accomplishment of any of His purposes: it is not to be expected that He will give more. Both these propositions flow at once from our conception of God as the Ruler of the Universe: the first, because we hold Him to be a *just* ruler; and the second, because we hold Him to be a *wise* one. They are also in accordance with religious experience in all ages, which pronounces that God does not do everything and leave to man nothing—does not take him to heaven against his will; but that at the same time those who put their trust in Him do in fact find grace and assistance in proportion to their need. Assuming then the truth of this twofold principle, let us proceed to apply it to the Inspiration of the Bible.

What then is God's purpose in giving the Bible? Surely that it may be an authentic record of His revelation of Himself to mankind; a supernatural history of the Supernatural. We should then expect, according to the principle just enunciated, that the supernatural element in this work of God's should extend so far as is necessary for this purpose, but no further. Let us then consider the Bible as if it were yet to be written, and inquire what measure of supernatural aid will be necessary to make it a true record of the Divine dealings with mankind. To ascertain this we must first consider the various classes of these dealings. They were as follows:—

i. Supernatural *Deeds* or miracles, such as e.g. the passage of the Israelites through the Red Sea, or the raising of Lazarus. Supposing such deeds to have been wrought, it is clearly of high importance that a true account of them should be preserved; especially as they constitute after all the most striking and unmistakable proof that there is such a thing as divine interposition in the affairs of men.

ii. Supernatural *Words* (i.e. Prophecy), forming a direct revelation of things known only to God, and not to be discovered by the unassisted power of man; such as the future of the individual and the race, Heaven and Hell, the Triune nature of the Deity, and so forth. This forms in effect the great message of the Bible, and is to be found there and nowhere else.

iii. Supernatural *Laws*, the Commandments given by God to man, to guide him towards that heaven which prophecy reveals, and to confirm and supplement those natural laws which are everywhere implanted in his heart.

iv. Supernatural *Arrangements*. By this term I understand those general dealings of God with nations or individuals, which are not in their *form* supernatural (following, as they appear to do, on mere natural laws or actions), but are so in their *substance*, inasmuch as they either carry out some direct warning or prediction of prophecy, or else enforce in some special manner the observance of divine law. A general type of such arrangements is the whole history of the Jewish people, as recorded in the Old Testament; much there recorded is not in itself supernatural, but yet "was written," as S. Paul expresses it, "for our learning, on whom the ends of the world are come."

Now, if the Bible is to fulfil its purpose, clearly it is *necessary* that each of these four classes of supernatural phenomena should be faithfully and distinctly recorded therein.

But how much does this necessity imply? What limitations are there which we may expect to find imposed upon the absolute fulness and perfection of the record, so that it will not go further than our principle of divine economy will allow? The answer to this question will be different according to the nature of the phenomena we are considering. Let us revert to the four classes just distinguished, and ask the question as to each of them separately.

(i) Divine deeds, or miracles. Now in these it is clear that what is of importance is the main fact, the supernatural intervention; the details accompanying it have probably in themselves nothing miraculous, and are not essential to the record. Hence we should expect that, while the central fact stood out clearly, and was the same in all records, the accompanying circumstances would be left to the ordinary powers of the several narrators; and would accordingly exhibit just those errors of detail and small divergencies in unimportant matters, which several accounts of the same transaction always contain, though related by faithful and careful historians. But it will be admitted on all hands that this is exactly the case with the Bible accounts of miraculous events. Take for instance the greatest of all miracles, that which is in fact the keystone of the Christian religion, — the resurrection of our Lord Jesus Christ. The four accounts which we have of this event and its consequences are entirely at one in their main features. From each of them we learn that it took place very early in the morning of the first day of the week; that the actual rising was unseen by any mortal eye; that the first appearance of our risen Lord was to some of the women who had approached the sepulchre with the loving intent of paying the last possible duties to their Master's body; that this was followed by isolated appearances to particular persons, and to the general body of the disciples;

finally, that, although He did not afterwards live constantly and familiarly among them as He had done before His passion, yet, as it is well summed up by S. Luke, "He showed Himself alive by many infallible proofs, being seen of them forty days, and speaking of the things pertaining to the kingdom of God." Of these main facts, then, we are sufficiently assured. But in the minor details, such as the much-vexed question of the exact number and order of the women who visited the tomb, there are apparent discrepancies and difficulties, which all the skill of harmonizers has been unable to remove. Nor, if our theory be correct, is there any need that we should remove them: they form no obstacle to a rational belief in Inspiration, while they give the best possible proof that the narratives containing them are not "cunningly devised fables," but genuine, and therefore slightly divergent records of a real historical fact.

(ii) Supernatural *Words*, or prophecy in the largest sense of the term. Here the case is different. Instead of a divine action recorded by a human historian, we have a divine message delivered through a human messenger. Here, as in all messages, accuracy is of the highest importance; not only accuracy in the main fact, but in the minutest terms and details. The only way in which it may vary is in accordance with the form in which the message itself was delivered. It seems probable, as we have seen above, that in many cases the divine communication took the form of a vision seen, not of words heard. The commencement of the prophecy of Isaiah may again be taken as a striking proof of this, "The vision of Isaiah the son of Amoz, which he saw . . concerning Judah and Jerusalem." And in the New Testament the book of Revelations is throughout a splendid example of the two forms of communication combined. Thus in the epistles to the seven churches we have spoken words, which we must expect to be literally delivered, as they were addressed to the apostle by his glorified Lord; but from thence he passes up into the courts of heaven, and proceeds to describe a series of scenes, evidently symbolical, the true meaning of which it was for the most part left both to him and his readers to gather for themselves. It is clear that in this latter case the writer can only describe in his own words the things which he has seen; consequently it is possible that slight mistakes or confusions, incident to such a descrip-

THE LIMITS OF INSPIRATION. 139

tion, may be met with; although clearly they must not be such as to interfere with the complete general truth of the picture.

(iii) Supernatural laws. Here it is the general sense or drift of the commandment that is essential; the exact words in which it is couched are of less importance. For we have now come down out of heaven, where everything is strange and must be exactly reported, and are again upon this earth, with which we are familiar. Of course the directions may in some cases be precise and minute, as in Leviticus, where a great number of positive enactments on ceremonial matters are given. But as a general rule, and especially in the New Testament, the precepts of the Bible are clearly intended, not to supersede men's conscience and moral judgment, but only to guide it; and they deal with principles rather than with details. Now, as few things are more fixed than the principles of morality, few things more variable than the manner in which they are applied in different places and times, we may expect that the writers of Scripture should be wholly at one, both amongst themselves and with the cultivated conscience of civilised man, on all the great and fundamental principles of morality and religion;

but that they may possibly fall short of the latter in their view of certain points of practical detail, which in their age had not been developed and insisted upon. Hence, for instance, may be explained the fact that S. Paul, whilst in many places he applies the principles of Christian charity to regulate the relations of master and slave, nowhere explicitly denounces the iniquity of holding slaves at all; a practice which in his day was an integral and unquestioned branch of political economy, though it was soon to wither and perish under the free air of Gospel truth.

(iv) *Supernatural arrangements.* These, as before explained, are actions in which we recognise the direct interposition of God, but only in so far as they are fulfilments of prophecy, or illustrations of principles which He has laid down. Here again it is only the main facts with which we are concerned; the details and accompanying circumstances are of still less importance than in the former case, having usually in themselves no religious or moral significance whatever. The historical books of the Old Testament are special instances of this class; and in these, while the march of events must be faithfully narrated and clearly laid down, we may expect that the connecting details should exhibit all the haziness and inaccuracy which is inseparable from human history in all its aspects. Least important of all these connecting links are those merely formal ones of dates, numbers, names, and genealogies. That these should be recorded may be desirable for the completeness of the history, but can hardly add in any way to its moral teaching or significance. Here therefore we should expect fewest traces, if any, of supernatural aid. And this exactly accords with the fact that it is precisely in these matters of dates, numbers, names, and genealogies that the chief " Bible difficulties " are found to reside. For example, the whole of Biblical chronology, and therefore the whole of the antagonism which is supposed to exist between its teaching and the science of geology, depends on one solitary passage of Genesis, that which is called "the generations of Shem" (Gen. xi. 10–26). This passage gives the names of the intervening links between Shem and Abraham, and the number of years which each lived before the birth of the son who continued the succession. These names are names and nothing more,—those who bore them are no otherwise known to us, therefore, we may presume, no otherwise deserving of record. Still less does the length of time which each lived, before and after the birth of his firstborn, possess, so far as we can see, the slightest significance, moral or otherwise, in the history of God's dealings with man. On the other hand, to a Jew it was a matter of high interest and importance that Abraham, the founder of his race, traced back his descent to Shem, the eldest son of Noah; and the more circumstantial the particulars of this descent, the more gratifying to his national pride. This is therefore exactly the place where we might expect some interpolation or amplification of the original text. Nor, on the principles here laid down, ought we to conclude that such an attempt would have been somehow frustrated by divine interposition. It is not necessary to suppose any deliberate forgery; the particulars may have been imported in good faith from some genuine, but inaccurate, record. Nor do I say that the assumption of such an interpolation would have been justified, so long as no counter evidence existed. We should accept the record, as we accept other records, as our best guide, so long as nothing exists to shake their authority. But the case is altered when the book of nature, which, even more directly than the Bible, is the Word of God, pronounces clearly against the exact truth of such a statement. I am not here giving an opinion whether, even in the case of the antiquity of man, this verdict is as yet a certain one. But, assuming it to be so, it is clearly our duty to accept God's truth, as "in sundry ways and in divers manners" He imparts it to us, and to resign our belief in the exact chronology of a record, which He gives no reason to believe is otherwise than touched with the necessary imperfections of human error.

The above sketch, which might be greatly amplified, is perhaps enough to show that the *phenomena* of the Bible are in accordance with the principle of divine economy, as we have formulated it. We proceed to inquire how far the *language* of the Bible, its own witness respecting itself, favours or hinders the establishment of the principle. We must recur to our list of passages bearing on Inspiration; and, as in all cases of theology, we must be content with scattered hints and references, and not expect formal statements of dogma.

It is clear from what has been said above that, if the principle be true, we must be able to recognise three distinct states of Inspiration in the writers of Scripture. These are the following:—

(i) *Direct Inspiration*, where the writer is merely transcribing an actual revelation from God, made immediately to himself; and even in the transcription has a supernatural power working in and controlling him.

(ii) *Indirect Inspiration*, where the same controlling power operates, but where the matter recorded, although supernatural, is known to the writer, mainly at least, by the ordinary channels of information. This matter may be either supernatural words (as in the case of Christ's discourses given in the Gospels), or else merely supernatural deeds, or arrangements; and the extent and nature of the controlling power will be different in these different cases.

To distinguish classes (i) and (ii), we may say briefly that the writer is in the first a *messenger*, in the second an *historian*.

(iii) *Preventive Inspiration*, where the matters are wholly within the writer's knowledge, and at the same time of no immediate supernatural import, being in general a mere filling in of details. Here the writer will be simply left to himself, to tell his story in his own way; and the only work of Inspiration will be to *prevent* the introduction of any serious error, such as could not be detected by the readers of later generations, and might produce evil results.

How far then can these three states of Inspiration be recognised in the various books of the Old and New Testament?

i. *Direct Inspiration.* So far as the Old Testament goes, this inquiry has been already made (p. 71). We have seen that the parts where it is to be looked for are chiefly the prophetical books; and that accordingly these do, in the strongest manner, announce themselves as being literal transcriptions of "the word of the Lord." In some cases the organ through which the message came to the prophet appears to have been the eye, in others the ear; in the first case he tells us of a "vision which he saw," e. g. Isa. i. 1; in the second, that "the word of the Lord came unto him," Hosea i. 1, &c. Again, from Jer. xxx. and xxxvi, it would appear that the message was in some cases written down as it was received, and first given to the world in a written form; in others it was first spoken, and afterwards written down, but still under the immediate command and guidance of the Lord Himself. Here then we have direct Inspiration strongly and frequently insisted on, just where we should expect to find it. In the New Testament the evidence is more scanty. It is true that there are passages, such as the words of the narrative of Christ's temptation, which must have had their origin, it would seem, in a direct revelation from God; but still there is no actual assertion of this kind anywhere in the Gospels or Acts. With S. Paul it is otherwise. In 1 Cor. ii. 13 he states that the Spirit teaches, not the substance only, but the very words which he utters, in preaching the mysteries of God. Again, 1 Cor. vii, which has been examined already at length, gives a strong, though indirect proof, that S. Paul believed himself to be speaking in general by "the commandment of the Lord." The same is shown by Eph. iii. 3; iv. 17; and Tit. i. 3; while in Gal. i. 12 we have once for all the distinct assertion that he was taught the Gospel "by the revelation of Jesus Christ." Several passages of Hebrews (iii. 7; ix. 8; x. 15) cite texts of the Old Testament as spoken "by the Holy Ghost;" and similarly 1 Pet. i. 11 speaks of "the Spirit of Christ" as being in the prophets, testifying and revealing. Still more clear is the Second Epistle of the same apostle, which, in i. 21, tells us that the prophets of the Old Testament "spake as they were moved by the Holy Ghost," while in iii. 2 the writings of those prophets and the commandments of himself and his brother apostles are placed on exactly the same footing. But the clearest marks of direct Inspiration are to be found just where we should expect to find them, viz. in the Apocalypse—the only book of the New Testament which belongs to the same class as the prophetical books of the Old Testament. It is the narrative of a vision, closely parallel to that contained in the opening chapters of Ezekiel. S. John expressly tells us that the occasion of the vision was when he was "in the Spirit on the Lord's day;" that he was taken up into heaven; and that his narrative is the description of the things which he had there "seen and heard," xxii. 8. How soon afterwards it was committed to writing does not appear; but we need not doubt that the same influence which vouchsafed the vision also presided over the record of it.

ii. *Indirect Inspiration.* This is pre-eminently the Inspiration of the Gospels; which record, not revelations directly made for the first time to the writer, but revelations contained in the words and actions of our Lord Jesus Christ. It is of course conceivable that they might nevertheless be repeated to the writers by a supernatural dictation; but this there seems no reason to believe. Two of the evangelists, S. Matthew and S. John, were apostles themselves; a third, S. Mark, is reputed to have been little more than an amanuensis to S. Peter. None of these give any hint as to the source of their information; which is exactly what we should expect, where the writers were known to have been eye-witnesses of the events they related. With the fourth, S. Luke, the case is different. He was neither an apostle nor even an immediate follower of our Lord. And it is he who does take pains to give us, in the introduction to his Gospel, an account of the reasons and the sources of its composition. Here however we find nothing about a specially vouchsafed revelation, such as would have given at once the ground and the sanction to the writing. Like any human historian, he gives, as the justification of his work, the need (already widely recognised) of framing a connected narrative of the great events of the Gospel; and, as the reason why his own narrative should be accepted, the fact that he had carefully traced out and followed up the march of events from the very first, so as to be able to record with accuracy all that had been delivered to the Church by those who had been "eye-witnesses and ministers of the word." It is clear therefore that we must not look here for *direct* Inspiration, but only for that guiding and modifying influence which would ensure that the record, though coming through human channels, should be in all essential points accurate and true. That this influence existed, and that it was the only influence, seems further made clear by three passages of S. John, viz. xiv. 26; xvi. 12, containing the promise of the Holy Spirit; and xxi. 24, in which the apostle seems to base his claim to be believed on the human grounds, that he was a trustworthy witness of things which he had seen and heard.

iii. *Preventive Inspiration.* Here we suppose the writer to be merely making statements on matters which were within his own knowledge and his own powers of verification. Here the Inspiration can only be supposed to extend to such a superintendence as to ensure that no serious or harmful error shall be introduced—it is thus negative, not positive. Evidences of this form of Inspiration are not rare in the New Testament. They may be classed under the following heads.

(1) *Quotations from the Old Testament.* Quotation is specially a case where a writer deals with matters wholly within his own knowledge. It is therefore remarkable, especially in contrast with the extreme deference paid in modern times to the exact letter of Holy Writ, how boldly and loosely the writers of the New Testament cite passages from the Old. So long as they preserved the spirit, they would seem to have been almost careless as to the words. It would appear too that they took little account of what we may term their Authorized Version, *i.e.* the Septuagint. Thus S. Paul quotes sometimes from this, sometimes apparently direct from the Hebrew, sometimes from neither. It is needless to examine the whole of the New Testament quotations to verify these statements, but we may select one or two examples.

In all three Synoptic evangelists (Matt. xi. 10; Mark i. 2; Luke vii. 27) we have a quotation of a most important passage in Malachi, iii. 1. In the first and third instance the words are given as from the lips of Christ Himself. And yet in all three cases we read "before Thee," instead of "before Me," as it stands in the Hebrew. The difficulties of this case, great as they are, may perhaps be explained, *e.g.* by the hypothesis that the alteration was designedly made by our Lord Himself: but it shows at least that strict accuracy in citation is not to be looked for.

There is again a well-known case in Matt. xxvii. 9, where "Jeremy the prophet" is stated to have spoken words really found in Zechariah (xi. 12). Various explanations have been suggested here also; but the general looseness of the citation, when compared with the original, seems strongly to support the view that it is a case of simple mistake: the evangelist quoted from memory, and without referring to a copy of the Prophets for verification. It is to be remembered that MSS. of the Hebrew Scriptures were not common, as books are now, and may have been difficult of access at the moment.

Again, in John vii. 38 ("as the Scriptures have said, out of his belly shall flow rivers of living water,") we have words of our Lord, spoken publicly in an assemblage of the Jews, and expressly stated to be a saying of Scripture; and yet there is the utmost difficulty in determining what passage they are intended to allude to:

Prov. xviii. 4 being the most probable. Certainly there is no passage which they accurately represent.

This looseness of citation is not confined to the Gospels. In Acts xv. 16, S. James, speaking at the Council of Jerusalem, quotes a passage from Amos (ix. 11), in a form very different from that which is found in the Hebrew. It is to be observed however that this is in the course of a speech, where exact citation is more difficult: and the same applies to the well-known difficulty in the speech of S. Stephen, as to the purchase of the sepulchre at Sychem (Acts vii. 16). S. Paul's practice, as I have already hinted, is still more uncertain. In Eph. v. 14 we have a citation "Awake thou that sleepest and arise from the dead," which it has been found very difficult to verify at all, and which is certainly inexact. In 2 Cor. vi. 17, 18 we have three passages, from Leviticus, Isaiah, and Jeremiah, apparently blended together. In Heb. viii. 9, which is a citation from Jer. xxxi. 32, the words of the Hebrew, "although I was an husband unto them," are changed to the very different form, "and I regarded them not." Lastly, taking the Apostolic Epistles, James iv. 5 "The spirit that dwelleth in us lusteth to envy," is another instance of a reference which it is exceedingly difficult to verify: and 1 Pet. ii. 6, "behold I lay in Zion a chief corner-stone, &c." varies considerably in language, if not in sense, from its source, Is. xxviii. 16.

These and the like variations have generally been accounted for by the supposition that the New Testament writers were inspired to throw the words of the Old Testament into a different shape, which brought home to their readers the real sense (or in many cases the secondary and mystical sense) more clearly than a mere literal citation. Without pronouncing on the merits of this hypothesis, I may remark that at least it goes to prove how little the mere words of Scripture are to be regarded in comparison with their signification. Further, if this hypothesis may serve to explain such distinct variations as in the citation from Malachi iii. 1, or the change in Heb. x. 5, of "a body hast thou prepared me," for "mine ears hast thou opened:" yet it is clearly inapplicable to slight variations and omissions such as in Heb. i. 6 ("angels of God" for "gods"), or 1 Pet. ii. 6—or to mistakes in fact, as Matt. xxvii. 9—or to passages which are so vaguely given that they cannot be found to any certainty, as Eph. v. 14; Jas. iv. 5. It seems clear that these errors could not have arisen if the writer had had the passage held as it were before his eyes, which the acceptance of the literal theory would require; and hence we must assume that the verification was left to themselves, as a task within the reach of their own unassisted powers.

(2) *Cases where we can see that the writer is thinking for himself;* i.e. where he is consulting his own memory, or his own judgment. This has already been fully discussed in Part II, p. 119, and need not here be enlarged upon.

(3) What are usually called the *Discrepancies* of the Bible—slight inaccuracies as to detail, or errors in matters of fact, such as always occur in the most faithful narration, and are rather a confirmation than a discredit to its general truth. On this head also it is needless to enlarge: since it has been treated with great fulness and clearness in Warington's work on Inspiration, and specimens selected from those he has quoted have already been given in Part II, p. 124.

A very few words will suffice to sum up this inquiry. In Part I we showed that the witness of the New Testament to itself did not support the Natural Theory, according to which there is no special or divine element in the Bible at all. In Part II we showed that the Literal Theory, according to which the divine element is everything, and the human element nothing, was equally unsupported by the facts. In this last part we have endeavoured to ascertain where, between these two limits, the true theory of Inspiration lies. We considered Warington's principle, that Inspiration extends to spiritual matters only, and showed that it was difficult both of proof and application. We then proposed the simpler principle that God will give all such aid as is *necessary* for the accomplishment of His purposes, but that He will not give more. In applying this principle to the phenomena of the Bible, we distinguished between the four classes of God's supernatural dealings with mankind—deeds, words, laws, and arrangements. We saw that in recording each of these there would be, according to the principle, certain special characteristics in the Inspiration; and that Inspiration would thus take three special forms, which we distinguished as direct, indirect, and preventive. Finally, we showed that these three forms were all to be traced in Scripture, and that the main phenomena of Inspiration were strictly in accordance with the theory.

On the whole, what has been said may perhaps be sufficient to show that the principle of Divine economy is capable of explaining, at any rate, the main phenomena of Inspiration, as presented by the New Testament. As the principle is itself one which no existing school of theologians would seem to deny, it may legitimately be accepted as offering a solution of the question; at least until the further progress of science and research shall reveal difficulties with which it is incapable of dealing.

APPENDIX.

List of Texts bearing upon Inspiration.

Matt. i. 22; iv. 4; iv. 7; iv. 10; iv. 14; v. 17; viii. 17; ix. 13; x. 19; xi. 10; xii. 40; xiii. 14; xiii. 35; xvi. 4; xvii. 11; xix. 4; xxi. 4; xxi. 42; xxii. 31; xxii. 43; xxiv. 37; xxvi. 39–44; xxvii. 9.

Mark vii. 6; xi. 17; xii. 10; xii. 26; xii. 29; xii. 35; xiii. 14; xv. 28.

Luke i. 3; ii. 37; iii. 16; iv. 4–12; iv. 21; vii. 27; xi. 30; xii. 12; xvi. 31; xix. 46; xx. 17; xx. 37; xx. 42; xxii. 37; xxiv. 25; xxiv. 44.

John ii. 7; ii. 17; v. 39; v. 46; vi. 19; vi. 45; vii. 38; x. 35; xii. 14; xiii. 18; xiv. 26; xv. 26; xvi. 12; xix. 24; xix. 28; xix. 36; xx. 9; xxi. 24.

Acts i. 16; i. 20; ii. 16; ii. 25; ii. 30; ii. 34; iii. 21; iv. 11; iv. 25; viii. 34; x. 33; xv. 13; xvii. 11; xx. 25; xxvi. 22; xxviii. 25.

Rom. i. 1; i. 17; iii. 2; iii. 10; iii. 20; iv. 3; iv. 7; iv. 17; viii. 36; ix. 13; ix. 15; ix. 25–33; x. 5–8; x. 11; x. 15; x. 19; x. 20; xi. 2; xi. 8; xi. 9; xi. 26; xii. 19; xiv. 11; xv. 3; xv. 9; xv. 21; xvi. 25.

1 Cor. i. 16; i. 19; i. 31; ii. 4; ii. 13; iii. 19; vii. 10; vii. 25; vii. 40; xiv. 21; xiv. 37; xv. 3; xv. 27; xv. 45; xv. 54.

2 Cor. iv. 13; vi. 2; vi. 16; viii. 15; xi. 3; xi. 17; xii. 1; xiii. 3.

Gal. i. 1; i. 12; iii. 8; iii. 10; iii. 11; iii. 13; iii. 19; iv. 21; iv. 27; iv. 30.
Eph. iii. 3; iv. 8; iv. 17; v. 14; vi. 2.
Col. i. 23–29.
1 Thess. ii. 13; iv. 1; iv. 15.
2 Thess. ii. 5; ii. 15; iii. 14.
1 Tim. iv. 1; v. 18.
2 Tim. iii. 14.
Tit. i. 2.
Heb. i. 1; i. 6; ii. 2; ii. 6; ii. 11; iii. 7; iv. 34; v. 5; viii. 7; ix. 8; x. 5; x. 15; x. 30; xii. 26; xiii. 5.
James ii. 8; ii. 23; iv. 5.
1 Pet. i. 10; i. 16; ii. 6.
2 Pet. i. 19; iii. 2; iii. 15.
1 John ii. 7.
Rev. i. 1; i. 10; ii. 7; xiv. 6; xiv. 13; xix. 9; xxii. 8.

OXFORD:

E. PICKARD HALL, M.A., AND J. H. STACY,

PRINTERS TO THE UNIVERSITY.

www.ingramcontent.com/pod-product-compliance
Lightning Source LLC
Chambersburg PA
CBHW020301170426
43202CB00008B/450